The Loyalist Mind

*This volume was published with the
cooperation and support of the Pennsylvania
Historical and Museum Commission in its
continuing attempt to preserve the history
of the people of the Commonwealth.*

The Loyalist Mind

Joseph Galloway
and the American Revolution

John E. Ferling

THE PENNSYLVANIA STATE UNIVERSITY PRESS
UNIVERSITY PARK AND LONDON

Library of Congress Cataloging in Publication Data

Ferling, John E
  The Loyalist mind.

Includes bibliography and index.
  1. Galloway, Joseph, 1731–1803. 2. American
loyalists—Biography. I. Title.
E278.G14F47   973.3'2'0924   77-22369
ISBN 0-271-00514-9

Designed by Gretl Yeager Magadini

Printed in the United States of America

Contents

Acknowledgments

The author of a historical monograph is indebted to so many persons that it is difficult for him to design a suitable order in which to express his gratefulness. Certainly librarians must be near the top of the list. I received considerable—and always considerate—assistance from the staffs at the Historical Society of Pennsylvania and the Library of Congress. But the librarians at West Georgia College bore the brunt of what must have seemed my endless requests, and they have earned my boundless gratitude.

Endeavors of this kind almost inevitably require financial assistance. I received handsome grants from the Learning Resources Committee of West Georgia College and the West Virginia Colonial Dames of America, for which I am most grateful.

Portions of this book first appeared in substantially similar form in articles, and are used here with the kind permission of the publishers. The articles were: "Joseph Galloway: A Reassessment of the Motivations of a Pennsylvania Loyalist," *Pennsylvania History*, XXXIX (Apr. 1972); "Compromise or Conflict: The Rejection of the Galloway Alternative to Rebellion," *Pennsylvania History*, XLIII (Jan. 1976); and "Joseph Galloway's Military Advice: A Loyalist's View of the Revolution," *The Pennsylvania Magazine of History and Biography*, XCVIII (Apr. 1974).

Numerous people have read and commented on various portions of this study. This list includes Edward Steele, W. Reynolds McCloud, and James Sefcik.

Three scholars deserve special thanks: William Painter, who, while I was an undergraduate, kindled my interest in history; E. Bruce Thompson, the historian who awakened my interest in scholarly research; and especially Elizabeth Cometti, without whose guidance, patience, and encouragement the study would never have been consummated.

The typing, proofreading, and occasionally even the editing of this study were undertaken cheerfully—no matter how great the crisis or how long the hours—by Vicki Ward and Donna Jon Powell.

Finally, my thanks to my wife Carol, who endured the sacrifices stoically and who expressed only encouragement at the endeavor; and to Inger, Alaric, and Bandit, who were at my side or on my lap through each draft.

Introduction

A man with the achievements of Joseph Galloway might, with some justification, expect a measure of worldly immortality. He might anticipate a city or county designated in his honor, or perhaps a university, a library, or a park endowed with his name. Galloway sat in the Pennsylvania Assembly for nearly twenty years, almost half that time as its Speaker. Only Benjamin Franklin, his close friend for all these years, was more important in his provincial political party. Galloway played a major role in the First Continental Congress and was elected to sit in the Second Congress. He was active in the American Revolution, effectively serving his commander as an intelligence official and writing more than a dozen pamphlets and books on the conduct of the war.

But today Galloway is seldom remembered, except perhaps by scholars or students who fleetingly encounter a textbook acknowledgment of the "Galloway Plan of Union." Galloway's misfortune was to choose the losing side during the Revolution. He remained a loyalist, a "Tory," as the rebels opprobriously labeled the counterrevolutionaries. A few months after resigning from the Continental Congress, Galloway was in General William Howe's camp assisting the British to crush the rebellion. Two years later he was in exile in London.

The prevailing image of Galloway is not flattering. During his lifetime he was subjected to attacks that would make even the most hardened contemporary public figure blanch. The earliest appraisals of Galloway were provided by political enemies who were hardly inclined to charity when evaluating loyalists. When the historian attempts to "decypher the doublings of cunning, and the duplicity of traitors," a rebel in British-occupied Philadelphia predicted in 1778, "he will select you, Galloway, from the group, as centering and involving in yourself the very essence of all *toryism* and villainy; and while he develops your character, drop a tear over the depravity of human nature." Another agitator represented Galloway as a man of "corrupted heart" who had consigned his "name to infamy" and his "soul to perdition." He was also depicted as the "cringing, bowing, sycophantic [Tory] who had a patent for manufacturing and retailing Intelligence Extraordinary for his Majesty. . . ."[1]

More often than not historians have been critical of Galloway. He has been described as a man with "traits of character which were far from admirable." Scholars have frequently noted his "well-known . . . haughtiness," his "disabling vanity." He was "cold and unbending" according to still another author. He "apparently had no sense of humor at all. He took himself and the world very seriously, never making light of any occurrence. . . . Galloway expected deference as a matter of course" so that "even his friends thought that he was arrogant, overbearing, and hot-tempered."[2]

These unsavory personality traits, it has been suggested, ultimately led to the undoing of Galloway. Arrogance left him "ill suited to [the] job of conciliation and persuasion" which he undertook on the eve of Anglo-American hostilities. Furthermore, with his "Tory oligarch's contempt for the necessities of practical politics," he "succeeded only in making the way easy for his enemies." Any man so aloof, another historian insisted, was of necessity "blind to reality" and incapable of fulfilling his political ambitions.[3]

But others have seen Galloway in a different light. An English friend found him to be a man of "solid Sense & thorough knowledge." Another acquaintance believed he was "much esteemed by the people." Some historians have depicted him as a "cultivated, responsible" statesman who manifested a "placid logic," and as "the most profound of all the American Tory thinkers."[4]

The essential Galloway, therefore, is not easy to discern. Today it is difficult, perhaps impossible, to arrive at a balanced portrait of Galloway. Few of his private papers survived the wartime destruction of his estate, so that he must be viewed almost entirely through the rather stilted, legalistic-sounding, one-dimensional public documents which have survived. The real man has vanished; the historian has been reduced to speculative inquiries and conjectures.

This study, however, seeks to discover a less elusive object, the mind of Galloway. Galloway was a prolific writer, a pamphleteer in Pennsylvania's rough and tumble political waters, an essayist in search of a means to escape the Anglo-American dilemma, a propagandist hoping to abort a revolt against Great Britain. Intellectual threads run throughout his three decades of political activism, often madly crisscrossing and careening into a jumbled, crazy-quilt pattern, but more often flowing into a coherent, discernible mosaic. This is the object to be scrutinized: the mind of a man who reached the pinnacle of power in his colony only to be toppled and driven into exile, the mind of a man who grasped many of the great concepts of his time, but who ultimately resisted the supreme political and intellectual phenomenon of his age.

Ideas, of course, cannot be separated from events. Therefore, the first section of this study will examine Galloway's behavior throughout the revolutionary years; the second section will investigate his ideology and the intellectual milieu in which he functioned.

I

A Loyalist and the Rebellion

*"the calamitous consequences
of your frenzy"*

1

Galloway and the Revolution:
"Retreat and Take Other Ground"

Joseph Galloway's ancestors immigrated to America from England after his great-grandfather attained a grant of land in Maryland from Lord Baltimore in 1662. Wise land investments and a lucrative family mercantile business elevated the Galloways to a prominent and comfortable position by the time Joseph was born in 1730. While he was still a small child, the family moved from Anne Arundel County in Maryland to Kent, Delaware, near Philadelphia. Galloway received no formal education, but after several years of private tutoring and a short period of study under an attorney, he moved to Philadelphia and was licensed to practice law. With his inherited wealth and a law practice which quickly flourished, Galloway ascended rapidly in Philadelphia society. In 1748 he was admitted to the elite Schuylkill Fishing Company, a fraternity of Philadelphia's most prestigious citizenry. Five years later he married Grace Growden, daughter of one of America's richest and most powerful men. Lawrence Growden owned a large iron manufacturing concern near Easton; he had served several terms as Speaker of his colony's Assembly and had sat on both the Supreme Court and Council of Pennsylvania. Moreover, as a wag remarked, Grace was one of the few unmarried ladies in the colony whose father possessed a four-wheeled carriage. Although raised a Friend, Galloway was married in Christ Church in Philadelphia following his conversion to Anglicanism. One of the most opulent families in Pennsylvania, the Galloways soon acquired a large house on Market Street in Philadelphia and five country estates, the largest of which—Trevose, in Bucks County—was originally part of the Growden estate.

Galloway's exalted status permitted him to play the role of gentleman farmer when not practicing law. His affluence enabled him to participate in the city's intellectual and scientific endeavors and, like many other wealthy Philadelphians, to speculate heavily in western lands. He and ten associates founded the Illinois Company in an attempt to acquire more than one million acres between the Mississippi and Illinois rivers. For a time he was president of the Indiana Company, which made purchases in the Ohio Valley. Later he and eight partners sought to purchase land between the Ohio and Tennessee rivers.

Little, however, is known of the man. His few surviving letters are largely political in nature and consist mostly of an occasional appeal to an ally or a short report on affairs of state to a distant friend. Even his letters to his wife reveal little, except perhaps indirectly. Much of this correspondence was terse, full of grumblings about the war or the conditions which beset the loyalist refugees. His communications disclose a total political being, a man immersed in public affairs. The letters also reveal a man unaccustomed to effusive affection. At most he could assure his wife that nothing "has given me so much peace as having you behind me."[1]

His daughter thought Galloway was a doting father, a man unselfish in the services he rendered to those who were less fortunate. His wife confided to the secrecy of her diary that Galloway "had his foibles but he was an honest Man." She thought him to be naive. "JG is two sanguin & these creatures Underminds him" repeatedly, she lamented. Even in times of great despair Galloway did naively persist in the belief that all would turn out for the best. "Injustice and Inhumanity never yet passed unrewarded," he counseled his wife. "Inhumanity can never prosper; . . . the Justice of a divine Providence will reward the Authors of it in due Time with the Measure it deserves." Nevertheless, despite an optimism about the eventual outcome of great events, his writings reveal a substantial distrust of the individuals with whom he dealt—a near paranoid impulse, in fact, to discern conspiracies and plots all about him.[2]

Galloway's abundant essays suggest a finely honed, legalistic mind. Each of his efforts, whether arguing questions of a constitutional nature or matters relating to the conduct of the war, was precise, lucid, organized. Each was a legal brief for the point he wished to make. His style was almost commonplace. The prose lacked the flair and adornment of the works of Thomas Paine or Samuel Adams; the deplorable redundancy which characterized many of the essays of James Otis and John Adams, however, was also absent.

Two etchings from original oil paintings of Galloway exist. One, probably made when he was about thirty years of age and near the pinnacle of political power and popularity, shows a man of genteel appearance. His features are soft, his eyes bright, alert, amiable. Still, his demeanor suggests nothing extraordinary. The artist depicted his subject in a manner similar to the paintings of the great majority of colonial nabobs. The second etching, almost certainly made when Galloway was in his mid-forties—and during a time of political and personal travail—reveals a character not given to ostentation. He appears to be strikingly lean. His features are sharp, his lips thin and tightly pursed. His eyes are slightly squinted, but expressionless. He appears rather unlined, although somewhat puffy about the eyes. In all, the portrait exudes the air of a man confident of his abilities, certain of his elevated stature—a man, despite the absence of frills, of hauteur.

Prepared in the law, well-received in the proper circles, so gifted an orator that he was acknowledged to be the "Demosthenes of Pennsylvania," and, finally, rich and prominent—his estate was once valued at £40,000—Galloway possessed all that was essential to enter the battleground of Pennsylvania politics.[3]

Pennsylvania traced its British roots to 1681, when the crown granted the region to William Penn as a proprietary colony. In 1701 Penn and the colonial assembly agreed to a Charter of Privileges which remained the constitution for Pennsylvania until the Revolution. The Charter, liberal in its grant of religious liberties but in no way extraordinary in its political ramifications, placed political power in the hands of a governor and council appointed by the proprietary family and in an elected assembly. Philadelphia, Chester, and Bucks counties were allotted eight seats each in the legislature, and the city of Philadelphia was awarded two representatives. The remaining ten seats were apportioned among the colony's western counties. The Charter further provided that the suffrage requirements should resemble those generally established throughout England. Voting was restricted to those males twenty-one years of age who accepted Jesus as a Savior, who had resided in the colony for two years, and who owned fifty acres of land or property valued at fifty pounds. In an agricultural society, few males, other than urban artisans, were disfranchised by the law.[4]

Nevertheless, it was uncommon for someone outside the rarefied social levels to actually wield political power. The nature of the Assembly's apportionment assured that political hegemony inevitably would be centered in the eastern regions of the colony. Two-thirds of the Assembly seats were filled by Philadelphia and its environs, although by the mid-eighteenth century that region contained only half the colony's population. Moreover, those qualified to vote in the East habitually returned their social superiors to the legislature.

A small, oligarchic clique of easterners, therefore, dominated the colony. Tied by religion, marriage, and economic interests, this elite divided into coalitions and grappled for dominance. The issues over which they struggled, however, were substantive and of interest to the entire colony. Problems of defense, Quaker domination, Anglo-American relations, and Indian policy predominated, but shrouding each of these issues were the critical questions of executive-legislative rivalry and local-versus-foreign governance.

One oligarchic faction, frequently referred to as the Old Party or the Quaker Party, traditionally controlled the Assembly. Well-disciplined and united, this party sought to resist executive encroachments on the legislative power. Early in the century the Quakers succeeded in making the Assembly nearly autonomous in matters of provincial finance and the formulation of Indian policy; and, throughout the colonial era, the party sought to perpetuate the privileged status of the colony's Quaker minority.

This faction's chief rival, contemptuously labeled the Proprietary Party by its foes, was a more informal collection of individuals and interests. Some of its members were sincerely interested in preserving proprietary government. Most merely hoped to terminate Quaker domination of the Assembly or perhaps to secure patronage favors as a reward for services rendered.

When Galloway took up residence in Philadelphia around mid-century, Pennsylvania's dominant political issue concerned military preparedness. The long struggle over this question ultimately provoked a restructuring of the political factions and catapulted both Franklin and Galloway into positions of preeminence. The colony's proximity to key Indian tribes, as well as to the western regions menaced by France, meant that Pennsylvania occupied a crucial strategic spot in Anglo-America. Military decisions undertaken in Philadelphia bore on the fate of all Britain's New World possessions. During the warfare early in the century, the Assembly held inflexibly to the pacifist dogmas of the Society of Friends and refused to expend even the smallest amounts for defense. The legislature once again assumed this position when King George's War erupted in the 1740s. Finally, years after the war commenced, the legislature, under severe British pressures, agreed to provide nonmilitary items to British troops. An unofficial association, led by Franklin, provided a voluntary militia for the defense of the colony.

Thoroughly exasperated at the prolonged intransigence of the Friends, Franklin had begun, by the early 1750s, to put together a new political faction built around his reputation and charisma and attractive to non-Friends who supported both military preparedness and legislative supremacy. The new coalition meshed when the French and Indian War began in 1755 on Pennsylvania's western frontier. Although many of the old pacifist arguments were once again rehearsed, the Assembly acted quickly to raise £60,000 in bills of credit for defense. Six Quaker assemblymen resigned rather than compromise their principles when Pennsylvania actually declared war on the Indians in June 1756. Their action provided the opportunity for Galloway to enter Pennsylvania politics.[5]

Galloway had begun to move into Franklin's orbit after 1750, probably as a result of a close friendship with the older man's son, William. Startling differences existed between Franklin and Galloway. Franklin, nearly twenty-five years older than Galloway, was extroverted, cosmopolitan, a newspaperman by trade, inventive, intensely interested in a variety of intellectual and scientific pursuits, and a deist in religious persuasion. Despite his assets, however, Franklin was victimized by a lower-class social background which obstructed his entrance into many of Philadelphia's elite positions. Galloway was less gregarious and more haughty, a lawyer, more commonplace in intellectual tastes and interests, an Anglican; but he was one of Pennsylvania's wealthiest inhabitants with all the proper connections. The two did embrace similar political philosophies and world outlooks. Both men cherished the empire, although both hoped that the imperial relationship would shortly be altered and reformed. Both men desired closer cooperation between the disparate colonies. Both men were alarmed at the deficiencies in proprietary government. Affection and respect existed on both sides, but essentially the two were allied out of convenience and opportunism. Franklin could assist Galloway's entrance into politics; Galloway could help secure Franklin's entry into the right circles.[6]

Franklin had reached the Assembly in 1751. Four years later Galloway came to his assistance by writing several vitriolic pamphlets and newspaper attacks on a political enemy. In 1756 Franklin, now political master of Philadelphia County, returned the favor and assisted in the election of Galloway to the Assembly. Subsequently he designated Galloway as his primary legislative assistant, and during the French and Indian War appointed him to the committee charged with prohibiting trade with the enemy and the committee to supply the militia. Shortly thereafter Galloway was named a member of the committee on Indian affairs and occasionally served as an Indian commissioner. When Franklin went to London for a five-year period beginning in 1757, Galloway took over many of his assignments, including a seat on the important committee on grievances.[7]

The long, tenuous relationship between the Pennsylvania executive and legislature burst into open, tumultuous conflict soon after Galloway became a member of the Assembly. The issue of proprietary taxes and the French and Indian War sparked the confrontation. The refusal of the proprietor, Thomas Penn, to pay duties on his Pennsylvania property had aroused the ire of the Assembly for some time, but when he refused to pay a wartime emergency levy on the family's estates the Assembly was beside itself with anger. Nevertheless, the legislature remained powerless to compel the proprietor to pay the duties. In 1757 Governor James Hamilton again rejected a similar land tax bill, provoking an Assembly remonstrance and street demonstrations.

Three months after Galloway's first election, therefore, the legislature sent Franklin to Great Britain to attempt to negotiate a compromise with the proprietor; failing that, Franklin was to request that the House of Commons compel the proprietary family to pay its taxes. Five years in London were unproductive, however, and Franklin returned home empty-handed in 1762. A year later the tide turned. The frontier flared again as still another Indian campaign engulfed Pennsylvania's western settlements. Once again a military appropriation bill fell victim to the executive-legislative deadlock over the question of the rights of the proprietors. Only a threatened siege of Philadelphia by desperate and anguished frontiersmen induced the frightened assemblymen to surrender and take swift action. The legislature not only hastily passed a defense measure, it decided the time had arrived to seek an end to the experiment in proprietary rule.[8]

In March 1764 the Assembly appointed an eight-member committee to prepare resolutions and petitions for the termination of proprietary government; Galloway was designated chairman of the body. Within two weeks the Assembly adopted twenty-six resolutions presented by the committee. The resolves blamed the military setbacks of the recent wars on proprietary government, maintained that unequal taxation was inevitable under such rule, claimed that the proprietors monopolized the best lands in the colony, and urged that royal government be permitted to supersede proprietary rule in Pennsylvania. To augment the royalization scheme, Franklin sailed once again for London.[9]

The Assembly action did not go unanswered. John Dickinson, an obscure member of the Proprietary Party, attacked the move to alter the colonial government. Although he did not defend the existing regime, Dickinson maintained that an anti-proprietary battle would cause disharmony within Pennsylvania at a time when "some late acts" of Parliament demonstrated that Britain was about to attempt substantial alterations within the empire. If divided, he asserted, the colony would be unable to protect its vital interests against parliamentary encroachment. If royalization occurred, Dickinson further warned, many of the rights and privileges which Pennsylvania had enjoyed under the Charter of Privileges might be lost.[10]

Galloway responded with an impassioned address to the Assembly. It was imperative, he argued, that action be taken immediately, or, through their wealth and power, the proprietors would fashion a network of allies in Pennsylvania which would be impenetrable in a few years. Moreover, he denied that Pennsylvania's charter privileges would be jeopardized by an alteration of government. Galloway admitted that the designs of the ministry were uncertain, but he believed Pennsylvania could expect "mild and equitable Measures" from London. Certainly, he added, royal government would be less tyrannical than proprietary rule. He defended the recently announced British decision to maintain troops in America and argued, as Franklin had, that the troops promised protection from both foreign and domestic malcontents. Galloway was anxious at the prospect of further domestic unrest and believed the recent march of frontiersmen on Philadelphia demonstrated the inability of the proprietors to suppress the colony's lawless elements. The Dickinson-Galloway clash provoked a lasting enmity between the two ambitious young politicians—a rivalry so bitter that at one point the two engaged in fisticuffs on the Assembly floor and later Dickinson challenged his protagonist to a duel.[11]

During these years Galloway also struggled to secure life tenure for Pennsylvania judges. After 1701 British judges could be removed from office only by the Parliament, but American judges maintained their positions at the pleasure of the executive of each colony. Galloway regarded this system as absurd. Of necessity, colonial judges accepted a servile status that was incompatible with true justice. A judge, he alleged, inevitably became a mere "Tenant at Will" of his executive master. Galloway was partially motivated by antipathy toward a system which made judges dependent on proprietary governors. However, he also hoped to establish a system of checks and balances in the colonies commensurate with that which existed in the parent state.[12]

Well before the period of colonial discontent with England, Galloway took the lead in seeking a liberalization of imperial trade and currency regulations. As early as 1758, he advocated that America be permitted to export grain to those countries of Europe which were not avowed enemies of Great Britain. Most mercantile prohibitions, he believed, simply gave "the dishonest Trader an Opportunity of making his Fortune while the honest man alone remains a Sufferer." Later he advocated free trade between the colonists and Spain. He and Franklin also sought to persuade Britain that the development of an American currency was in the best interests of the empire. They argued that if the scarcity of money continued America would be unable to afford Britain's manufactured items; the colonists would then be forced to begin manufacturing their own goods. Curiously, he believed that an accumulation of money would enhance the agrarian way of life: "Let us have Money and we shall never think of Manufacturing or if we do, we shall never be able to perfect it to any Degree." He assumed that America, lacking a sufficient force of trained labor, could not compete with Britain and that the currency would contribute only toward making consumers of the colonists. In 1766 he drafted a petition to Parliament which requested more liberal imperial currency policies, and the following year he helped draft a bill—subsequently passed by the Assembly and upheld in London—which authorized the printing of indented bills in Pennsylvania.[13]

Galloway's role in the anti-proprietary struggle was not wholly altruistic. While he desired the termination of proprietary rule out of deep conviction, he also realized that he could personally profit from royalization. Rumor was rife in Philadelphia in the 1760s that Franklin hoped to become the colony's first royal governor and Galloway its first chief justice. Galloway's letters lend substance to the allegations.[14]

Galloway sustained his initial political setback in 1764. During a bitter, scurrilous election campaign, he failed for the first time—and the only time during his career—to secure reelection to the legislature. Out of over 3,800 votes cast in Philadelphia County, he fell eight votes short. The gratifying fact that he had outpolled Franklin must have been outweighed by the unpalatable news that Dickinson had been elected. The results were peculiar, for the Franklin-Galloway Party otherwise held its own. A well-orchestrated and vicious pamphlet campaign which the proprietary forces waged against the two leaders probably bore fruit, although the election indicated that the voters were not yet hostile toward an anti-proprietary movement.[15]

Meanwhile, other ominous storm clouds were gathering. Evidence now exists that Great Britain had quietly begun to reconstruct its empire as early as the 1740s. This policy shift at first produced only minor ripples of colonial unrest; few contemporaries perceived the subtle shifts in imperial policy, and Britain hastily abandoned its scheme when the French and Indian War erupted in 1754. Following the successful conclusion of the war, the ministry publicly announced its intention to initiate wide-ranging imperial reforms. Several considerations moved London to act. British officials had grown increasingly apprehensive at the recurrent, and frequently violent, domestic upheavals within the colonies. Moreover, the seeming inability of royal officials to govern in the colonies caused no small distress in Britain. Some in London were alarmed at the enormous growth among the Americans; many officials believed the colonies would seek independence if their expansion continued unabated. America's repeated reluctance to contribute money and men during the chronic colonial wars further antagonized the parent state.[16]

Consequently, in 1763 the ministry announced that a royal fleet and British army were to remain in America during peacetime. The government dispatched additional customs officers to the colonies and instructed the governors to rigorously enforce all British legislation. A royal proclamation prohibited westward migration beyond the Appalachians. The Sugar Act of 1764 increased the list of goods which could be shipped from America only to other parts of the empire and, of greater moment, attempted to raise revenue through the imposition of import duties on numerous items. In 1765 Parliament passed still another revenue-raising measure, the Stamp Act.

Historians have generally portrayed Galloway's behavior during the ensuing decade of crisis as opportunistic. He has usually been depicted as timid and as an equivocator, as a leader without great convictions. Some have argued that first he defended the British, then he endorsed the colonial position, and ultimately he sided with the imperial authorities. He was, according to a recent study, "a discreet sidestepper" who "was never quite certain what his position ought to be, and until 1776 he was reluctant to make a firm, final commitment."[17]

These conclusions have contributed to a misunderstanding of Galloway. He was, as several scholars have ably demonstrated, a prudent and sagacious politician who sensed private advantage in the course he pursued. That he might have hoped for political advancement as a result of his activities should hardly be surprising. It would have been remarkable for a politician of twenty years to be without political ambition. But such traits should not be taken to mean that he was without convictions, or that his actions were divorced from his philosophical concepts. Nor was he an un-principled, timid equivocator. Although his tactics changed as events dictated, his conduct remained remarkably consistent throughout the crisis.

Since well before the American upheaval which the Stamp Act provoked, Galloway, like imperial officials in London, had plumped for reform within the empire. Of course, the changes the provincial-minded Galloway hoped for hardly transcended the boundaries of his own colony. He sought to replace proprietary government with royal rule, to secure justices with life terms for the colonies, to mitigate Britain's mercantile yoke over the colonies. Galloway's first concern after 1765 was that these policies not be jeopardized by the upheaval. But as greater questions arose and as the impasse hardened, Galloway began to enunciate a more formal and more full-blown imperial ideology.

Although aware of the empire's problems, he had not developed a consistent philosophy of imperial constitutionalism before 1765. His provincial policies as well as certain legislative committee assignments occasionally brought him into contact with questions of Anglo-American relationships, but he was more concerned with purely local issues. He was certainly not alone in this respect. Only a trickle of pamphlets before the Stamp Act had dealt with questions of American rights in the empire. No direct evidence exists that Galloway studied any of these musings. For Galloway, as for most of his insular contemporaries, provincial issues were of paramount importance. Nevertheless, once imperial tensions were provoked, Galloway—without equivocation—argued persistently for the necessity of instituting changes within the empire and unswervingly urged the perpetuation of the Anglo-American relationship.

When news of the proposed Stamp Act reached America, Galloway's first concern was that Pennsylvania remain tranquil. He was a conservative who feared and deplored upheaval. Moreover, he thought that acceptance of the legislation would afford the best prospect for protecting his pet projects, particularly the anti-proprietary scheme. The October canvass was very much on his mind; after seven years in the Assembly he had been turned out of office in the preceding election. Tranquillity, he believed, would provide the best assurance for his election in 1765. Nevertheless, the ideas he developed throughout this first foray into the unexplored world of imperial constitutionalism closely resembled the philosophy he had already begun to enunciate as a provincial politician. Although his ideas were subsequently refined and honed, they were never substantially altered.

By the time Galloway spoke out, his faction was in great difficulty. Franklin had been publicly attacked as a turncoat for having defended the Stamp Act before the House of Commons. Pamphlets had appeared throughout America which condemned the legislation as a violation of the colonists' right to autonomously exercise certain legislative prerogatives. The opposition group in Pennsylvania, the Proprietary Party, utilized this turn of events to forestall, and perhaps prohibit, a change in the colony's form of government. The proprietary group charged that the Franklin-Galloway clique was attempting to surrender Pennsylvania to the very group in London which sought to destroy colonial liberties.

Galloway published his ideas on the Stamp Act in August 1765 in the *Pennsylvania Journal*. He argued that Britain, largely as a consequence of having to bear the cost of imperial defense, was in such deep financial trouble that many judicious persons had predicted the ruin of the empire. He felt that Americans were important contributors to England's plight because, while Britain had dispatched regulars to America to expel France and Spain from the continent, the colonists had contributed little to the success of imperial aims. Moreover, it was to British solicitude that the colonists owed their "present freedom from Indian barbarities, popish cruelties, and superstition." As an "infant state," Galloway continued, America still required British protection. Would anyone "be so absurd as to deny the reasonableness, the *necessity*, of the crown having some *certainty*" that America would henceforth help meet the financial burdens of military assistance? Britain's colonial competitors were hoping that America would refuse to assist the parent state, he advised, because this remained "the only foundation of their hopes of reducing the British dominions."[18]

Neverthless, Galloway acknowledged, the crucial problem raised by the stamp duties was not that of procuring revenue for military preparedness, but of fixing responsibility for levying the taxes. He believed that taxation enacted by the American legislatures offered the best assurance for the maintenance of colonial rights. However, if the military situation remained grave, and the American willingness to grant assistance to Britain continued to be so fickle, he concluded that it would become the "indispensable duty of a British parliament to interfere, and compel [America] to do what is reasonable. . . . " In short, the sovereign position of Parliament might compel it to act during an imperial emergency. Galloway did envision one alternative to British coercion. He recommended the creation of an American legislature which might conceive some plan to assert America's right to tax itself and to guarantee Britain that the colonies would indeed provide the necessary revenue. He had, therefore, proposed two means to end the crisis and preserve the empire. The colonies could accept the sovereignty of Parliament. Better still, the colonists might institute some quasi-legal—perhaps even illegal—body to propose major reforms in the exercise of power within the Anglo-American union. Regardless of the route the colonists took, the matter of greatest importance was that America not leave the shelter afforded by Great Britain. The colonies could not yet survive in a world of hostile nation-states. Whether America chose acquiescence or reform, he insisted, the solution must acknowledge British preeminence.[19]

Galloway's ideas were greeted with abuse. For several years his enemies referred to him as "Americanus," the sobriquet he used in signing the essay. His ideas, in fact, were not as reactionary as his enemies insisted. Although in private he admitted the reasonableness of parliamentary taxation, he stopped short of such sentiments in public by calling for voluntary American appropriations. Moreover, he had urged that the necessary taxes be passed by the Pennsylvania Assembly, and he had even called for an American congress—a body certain to be viewed as illegal by the government in London—to find a means around a parliamentary tax.[20]

However, the views of Galloway and his Pennsylvania adversaries had begun to diverge in two critical areas. Three weeks after the publication of his essay, the Pennsylvania Assembly passed a series of resolutions which attacked the constitutional basis of Parliament's powers of taxation. The Assembly's objections to the Stamp Act were couched in philosophical terms and based on a constitutional and natural rights philosophy. The colonists, the Assembly argued, were entitled "to all the Liberties, Rights, and Privileges of his Majesty's Subjects in *Great-Britain*, or elsewhere," including the right to be taxed only by one's elected representatives. Taxes levied by any legislature other than the colonial assembly were therefore "subversive of public Liberty." The Assembly, hence, denied the right of Parliament to tax America because the colonists were not, and could not adequately be, seated in its chambers and because Britain had long ago agreed to permit the Americans to tax themselves. Galloway insisted that unless the imperial constitution was reformed and the issue of sovereignty clarified, Parliament—as the heretofore clearly recognized sovereign imperial legislative entity—must be permitted to continue its powers of taxation. Even so, the Assembly, like Galloway, raised no questions about the right of Parliament to requisition monies and even promised to "cheerfully and liberally" meet all requisitions which "shall be called [for] . . . in a constitutional way."[21]

The ideas of Galloway and those of many colonists had begun to differ in another manner. Galloway remained the imperialist; his adversaries, their fondness for the parent state waning, were becoming American nationalists. Whereas Galloway scolded the colonists for their failure to participate fully in the recent colonial warfare, others were troubled by the implications of the seemingly perpetual imperial turmoil and by the niggardly benefits the colonists secured from the bloodshed. Dickinson, for instance, derided Galloway's point of view. America, he argued, had been dragged into wars fought solely for the benefit of Great Britain. Others denied Galloway's allegation of colonial slacking. The colonists, according to a New Englander in 1765, had cheerfully complied with each royal request, yet they reaped no advantages from the imperial conquest of America. The idea that America had aided Britain in defeating France and Spain, yet had never received adequate imperial assistance in the subjugation of its real enemy—the American Indian—became widely accepted. The colonies, it was also said, had been founded by private enterprise and not, as Galloway contended, by the largess of Great Britain.[22]

Instead of the tranquillity he had hoped for, Galloway now found Pennsylvania torn asunder and his political future in jeopardy. During the summer of 1765, mobs took to the streets terrifying those suspected of harboring a fondness for the Stamp Act. The property of Galloway, as well as that of Franklin and other leaders of the Assembly Party, was targeted for destruction. But Philadelphia, largely because of the unequivocal action taken by Galloway, was spared the mob violence which swept over many colonial urban centers. Galloway called upon the White Oaks—a formal organization of shipwrights which he and Franklin occasionally mobilized as a defense corps during periods of rowdyism—to assist in the preservation of order. In addition, he formed the Association for the Preservation of the Peace. Both organizations were ready, if necessary, to meet force with force. Intimidated by Galloway's eight hundred "sober inhabitants," the radicals "quietly retired."[23]

The crisis was not yet over, however, since the Assembly elections were near at hand and the Stamp Act, which had produced so much turmoil, was scheduled to take effect on 1 November 1765. The election, in spite of Galloway's anxiety, was rewarding. The Assembly Party won an overwhelming victory and increased its control over the legislature; Galloway received nearly five hundred more votes than in the previous election and regained the seat he had lost in 1764. Moreover, Galloway must have been delighted at the defeat suffered by Dickinson. Strengthened by his election victory and flushed with his recent success in preserving the peace, Galloway pushed for British repeal of the troublesome legislation. His action was not inconsistent with his behavior during the early days of the crisis; he had always, he privately told William Franklin, advocated the repeal of the Stamp Act. He therefore wrote a petition on behalf of Philadelphia's merchants which labeled the act "unconstitutional and very oppressive." The petition predicted that the stamp tax would drain off colonial specie. Galloway also wrote Franklin and Richard Jackson, the two agents representing Pennsylvania in London, and urged them to appeal to the British merchants to pressure the ministry for repeal. This appeal, he thought, should be based on the thesis that the Stamp Act was detrimental to Anglo-American commerce. He then issued a broadside asserting that his "Americanus" essay had been misconstrued and that he had never championed the Stamp Act. A few weeks later, news reached Philadelphia that the Stamp Act had been repealed.[24]

The Stamp Act furor had reaffirmed Galloway's belief that the colony required royal government. The proprietary leadership, he believed, had once again proven itself incapable of suppressing domestic violence. Furthermore, he insisted, the defenders of the Penn regime were the real instigators of the turmoil; the proprietary faction had conspired to defy Parliament and the crown as a ploy, deviously undertaken, to destroy the masses' attachment to royal rule. The Stamp Act turbulence, however, left Galloway in a quandary. Stringent defense of British policies involved immense domestic political dangers; criticism of British actions involved risking the ill will of influential ministers and jeopardizing the anti-proprietary struggle.[25]

Galloway therefore was alarmed when Great Britain announced a new colonial levy shortly after the repeal of the Stamp Act. In 1767 Parliament enacted the Townshend Duties, a tax on certain items imported by the colonists. Galloway regarded the duties as particularly troublesome and wished they "had never been thought of." But he also believed they might be turned to the advantage of the anti-proprietary faction. By raising the necessary revenue to pay the salaries of the colony's executive and judicial officials, the act might lessen the Assembly's control, as well as the control of Galloway's party over those leaders. The Penn family would thenceforth appoint officials without obligation who were funded out of the public treasure; furthermore, Galloway reasoned, since the proprietary interest clashed so often with that of the average citizen, it followed that the people would be less contented than previously. In addition, he believed the crown would not long tolerate a policy which permitted privately appointed officials to draw a public salary, and that if the colonists did nothing to anger the mother country, England would shortly royalize Pennsylvania.[26]

Thus in an anonymous newspaper essay, Galloway declared the taxes to be fair and legal, and he characterized the duty on tea as an "abundant favour" since it reduced the price of that commodity. He denied that the duties amounted to taxation without representation because it "lies at last at every ones *option* to take the commodity with the additional onus." However, as opposition to the taxes increased and Pennsylvania once again faced the prospect of upheaval, Galloway returned to the position he had taken in 1765. He supported an Assembly resolution which urged that Pennsylvania's agents in London seek repeal of the injurious duties, and in a second newspaper essay he defended the Massachusetts condemnation of the taxes. But Galloway was unwilling to support a nonimportation agreement, a move the Philadelphia radicals hoped to introduce as an economic weapon. His opposition was based on strategic and philosophic grounds. The boycott, he feared, would spawn deprivation and lead in turn to tumultuous riots; at stake were the anti-proprietary movement and the political monopoly of the colony's eastern oligarchy. Franklin, however, endorsed the boycott, leaving Galloway isolated. Rather than split the Assembly Party, Galloway chose to remain silent. A timely "sunstroke" kept him out of beleaguered Philadelphia until the crisis had passed.[27]

Although Parliament repealed the Townshend Duties in 1770, the initial five years of the imperial controversy had made a substantive impact on Galloway's career. Despite assurances that the prevention of violence since 1765 met "with his Majesty's Approbation" and Lord North's expression of high "regard for Pensilvania, which had behaved so well in all the late Disturbances," the proprietary government remained unmolested by London. In fact, a Privy Council decision not to recommend royal government for Pennsylvania—a decision made in 1765— probably sealed the fate of the anti-proprietary movement. Galloway foolishly continued to press for a hopeless cause, partially out of political naivete, partially because he was deluded by the false optimism manifested in Franklin's letters from London. Galloway might have disengaged himself from this disastrous policy had Franklin provided more accurate information from London. Franklin seems to have known by 1765 or 1766 that royalization was a chimera, but he misled Galloway into believing that Britain would shortly topple the proprietary interests if only the colonists would behave. If Pennsylvania behaved prudently, he told his friend, the colony would secure the end of proprietary rule. Although the colonies were "generally out of favor at present," Franklin informed his correspondent in 1766, the proper American conduct would ultimately secure ministerial reforms. There "are favourable Symptoms of the present Disposition of Parliament towards America, which I hope no Conduct of the Americans will give just Cause of altering." Even as late as 1773, Franklin exuded optimism, so that a provincial like Galloway might have believed London would soon begin an anti-proprietary reform program. "It is said," Franklin reported, that "there is a disposition to compose all differences with America" during the next few months. He also predicted a British war with its continental rivals in the near future. In such an event, the ministry would be compelled to take a conciliatory position with the colonists and all "our grievances would be redressed, and our claims allowed. And this will be the case sooner or later." Only much later, once the Anglo-American war had commenced, did Galloway come to regard Franklin as an untrustworthy person of great intrigue, an "ungrateful enemy to his country."[28]

Exposed and vulnerable, Galloway was severely damaged when the Secretary of State for the Colonies, Lord Hillsborough, dispatched a Circular Letter in April 1768 which denounced the colonists' conduct. Hillsborough, speaking for the ministry, threatened dissolution of those colonial assemblies which continued to oppose the Townshend Duties. The Circular Letter made a mockery of Galloway's assurances that royal government would be more accommodating than proprietary rule. Moreover, in August 1768 Hillsborough announced that Britain definitely would not royalize Pennsylvania. The despondent Galloway privately lamented that it was discouraging to those who had labored in behalf of the mother country to witness the rejection of such an "honourable and Beneficial" undertaking.[29]

Galloway's prestige was further diminished by a silly public quarrel with a Philadelphia editor. In 1767 Galloway, Franklin, and Thomas Wharton established a newspaper, the *Pennsylvania Chronicle*, which they hoped would be recognized as the official organ of the Franklin-Galloway faction in the Assembly. They also hoped the new journal would counter two radical Philadelphia papers, the *Pennsylvania Gazette* and the *Pennsylvania Journal*. The trio of financiers hired William Goddard, an experienced New Haven and New York publisher, and made him editor and owner of one-third interest in the venture. Despite the newspaper's motto, "Blessed the age in which one can think what he pleases and say what he thinks," the owners and editor soon quarreled over what was to be printed. When the editor published an attack on the Townshend Duties penned by Dickinson, Galloway immediately withdrew his financial support. Goddard retaliated by publishing a devastating pamphlet in which he accused his financial backers of being "men who were enemies to their country." "Mr. Galloway," he charged, "ridiculed my notions about liberty and the rights of mankind, and observed that 'the people in America were mad.' " He accused Galloway of harboring an anti-German animus, of assuming authoritarian powers in the Assembly, and of endeavoring to enslave his fellow countrymen by capitulating to Britain's every whim.[30]

During the early stages of the imperial crisis, Galloway had accurately reflected the temper of Philadelphia. By adroitly suppressing the potential violence in 1765, for instance, he enhanced his standing. The annual elections between 1766 and 1768 further strengthened Galloway— in the last canvass he garnered more votes than any other Assembly Party candidate. Dickinson, who had become well known the previous year through the publication of his *Letters from a Farmer in Pennsylvania*, even failed to win election to the legislature. But Galloway began to fade in 1769. Six candidates—all men who had openly encouraged nonimportation to force repeal of the Townshend Duties—gathered more votes than Galloway. The moderate policy of compromise cost him the support of Philadelphia's mechanics and artisans, and after 1770 he was compelled to seek election to a rotten borough seat in safe and rural Bucks County.[31]

By 1772 Galloway was so despondent that he seriously considered retirement from politics. But, perhaps as a result of soothing letters from Franklin, he ultimately sought reelection to the Assembly. Franklin urged Galloway to remain in the legislature "where your abilities are so useful and necessary in the service of your country. We must not in the course of public life expect immediate approbation and immediate grateful acknowledgment of our services. But let us persevere through abuse and injury . . . and [trust that] time will do us justice. . . . "[32] Later Franklin told Galloway that he was

> yet a young man, and may be greatly serviceable to your country. It would be, I think, something criminal to bury in private retirement so early all the usefulness of so much experience and such great abilities. The people do not indeed always see their friends in the same favorable light; they are sometimes mistaken, and sometimes misled, but sooner or later they come right again and redouble their former affection. This, I am confident, will happen in your case. . . . Therefore, preserve your spirits and persevere, at least to the age of sixty.[33]

Despite his occasional setbacks and moods of black despair, Galloway continued to possess significant power within his party. He was persistently reelected to the Assembly and in 1768 was chosen its Speaker—a post he retained, except for one term when plagued by illness, until 1774. His prestige, moreover, was acknowledged in 1769 when the College of New Jersey conferred upon him an honorary Doctor of Laws degree.[34]

During the three years of tranquillity between repeal of the

THE LOYALIST MIND

Townshend Duties and enactment of the Tea Act in 1773, Galloway, depressed and frequently ill, remained at Trevose for months on end. He came to Philadelphia only as business required and for the brief annual legislative session over which he presided. Galloway's despair was not unfounded. He realized that the Assembly Party tottered on the verge of deterioration. A breach existed within the very leadership of the Party, for Franklin had cautiously but gradually listed toward the policies of the radicals. Franklin's position on imperial questions after 1767 had been closer to that taken by Dickinson than to that which Galloway had advocated. Moreover, the Party was in serious difficulty in Philadelphia County, one of the first bastions of the eastern oligarchy. By 1771 the Party in that county could depend on only about twenty-five per cent of the votes it had annually polled before the Stamp Act crisis. Worn and haggard, old beyond his forty-odd years, Galloway must have seen that he faced a struggle to retain his power. He realized, his behavior seems to suggest, that the goals he had pursued for nearly two decades were now irrevocably beyond his grasp.[35]

Not even the news of a new parliamentary tax for the colonies could shake Galloway from his lethargy. Despite the enactment of the Tea Act of 1773, a measure designed to procure revenue through taxes placed on the sale of that commodity in the colonies, he remained inactive for nearly a year and at arm's length from the crisis that swirled about his colony.

Strong opposition to the tea legislation crystallized first in Massachusetts. The initial phase of the protest culminated in the destruction of British tea in Boston in December 1773, an action which induced Parliament to invoke the Coercive Acts against the recalcitrant New Englanders. At first Philadelphia remained calm. No "tea party" occurred; no British tea was sold. By May 1774, however, the radicals were organized and ready to assist beleaguered Boston, by legal means if possible, by illegal means if necessary. The radicals hoped to make the Assembly, of which Galloway remained the Speaker, the legal apparatus for assisting Boston.

Events compelled Galloway to act, but when he finally responded to the crisis he plunged unhesitatingly into the treacherous waters of Anglo-American politics. His isolation at Trevose had afforded him the opportunity to meditate on imperial relations and to structure the bits and pieces of his philosophical outlook. Although his attitude had not changed substantially since the Stamp Act controversy, it had been clarified and systematized. The decade of turmoil, the deterioration of his own position, the alarming events which followed the enactment of the Tea Act, awakened him to the realization that a full-blown revolution was possible—a debacle which would imperil the entire fabric of American and imperial life. He was aware that responses in both Britain and the colonies had polarized and that an impasse had developed.

The two countries had taken irreconcilable positions, he believed; unless each party agreed to compromise, hostilities were unavoidable. The British position—which he thought was "attended with more Mischief than Benefit"—was that "parliamentary Jurisdiction ought to be exercised over near 3,000,000 of People, none of whom have the least Participation in that Jurisdiction, or any Opportunity of communicating their Desires, Wants, and Necessities to it. . . . " The "American Advocates [denied] the constitutional Authority of the British State to bind the Colonies, because they were not expressly represented in her Councils." Moreover, the Americans declared that they would not accept such representation should it be offered. Both countries, he concluded, "should retreat a little, and take other Ground," for unless a compromise was reached quickly one of the antagonists was likely to seek a solution through force.[36]

It was hardly strange for Galloway to think in terms of compromise. The most talked about scheme for the reconstruction of the empire before the eruption of Anglo-American difficulties had come from Benjamin Franklin, Galloway's mentor. Franklin's Albany Plan of 1754 would have united the diverse colonies under one American legislature and English-controlled governor. Galloway had frequently sought compromises in the earlier confrontations, and he had championed the idea of an American congress as early as 1765. As the crisis intensified in 1774, more compromise solutions were discussed and some were published in Philadelphia.[37]

Galloway believed that any proposal for compromise must come from America, not from London, because the colonists were "inferior and the Party who sought Redress." The onus for causing or preventing a rebellion, he thought, lay with the colonists. He repudiated several popular notions as means of solving the impasse. He felt that seating colonists in Parliament would be unworkable because the proposal lacked support in both countries. Moreover, he urged that the colonists not resort to coercion, mob violence, or nonimportation agreements in an attempt to break the will of England. Such tactics could not weaken a people as powerful as the English, and they might provoke British retaliation. He regarded legal petitions for redress of grievances as the best means of securing negotiation, and he continued to insist that a national congress was a suitable body for drafting such a colonial appeal. While a congress had to be approached with trepidation, he had come to believe that only a national body was capable of resolving the crisis. Congress could overcome extremist dissension, he believed, and present the facade of an America unanimously seeking to compromise.[38]

In addition, Franklin may have led Galloway to believe that Great Britain was prepared to accept a compromise proposed by an American. As imperial troubles mounted after 1765, Franklin often advised Galloway that the British were anxious to discover some solution for the ills of the empire.

Franklin hinted at the British "disposition to compose all differences with America." Once he lamented that "a Cry begins to arise, Can no body propose a Plan of Conciliation?" When Galloway told Franklin in 1765 of a plan he had concocted which might reconcile America to Britain, Franklin excitedly promised to support any proposal his friend submitted. Franklin insisted that with "nobody here caring for the Trouble of thinking on't," the door was ajar for Galloway to offer his proposal. He advised Galloway that he "would try anything . . . rather than engage in a war" with Britain. The old sage recommended that Galloway not hesitate to champion unpopular policies. "Dirt thrown on a Mud-Wall may stick and incorporate," Franklin counseled, but it will "not long adhere to polish'd Marble."[39]

During the summer of 1774 Galloway threw off his lethargy and acted boldly. In mid-May the New York Committee of Correspondence called for an intercolonial congress to consider the proper American response to the Coercive Acts. Some members of this committee feared that another colonial boycott of British goods would provoke hostilities; others were reluctant for New York to take any action without broad national support. On 8 June a mass meeting in Philadelphia endorsed the idea of a national meeting and urged the colony's Assembly to select delegates to the congress. When the Governor failed to immediately convene the Assembly, another meeting ten days later—attended by eight thousand persons— urged the convocation of a provincial congress which might elect and instruct delegates to the congress. At this point Galloway acted. He urged his old enemy, Governor John Penn, to call the Assembly into session. Galloway favored a national meeting, but he hoped the delegates would be chosen by the more moderate Assembly. In mid-July the Assembly met. Galloway greeted the assemblymen with a speech urging the election of delegates to a national congress. He had fervently hoped, he told the legislature, that the defense of American rights might be undertaken by each colony. Unfortunately, action by individual colonies would not procure redress, and it might increase the danger of domestic violence and confrontation with the parent state. But a continental congress might recommend some solution which could establish a lasting political union between the two countries. The Pennsylvania Assembly agreed to the congress. It elected Galloway and six of its members as congressmen, thus rejecting the delegates elected by the provincial congress, and requested that he draft instructions for the colony's delegation. Galloway's advice to his fellow congressmen—advice which was remarkably similar to that given most delegations—was that the congressmen adopt a plan which would secure the rights of the colonists and establish "that Union and Harmony which is most essential to the Welfare and Happiness" of Britain and America.[40]

The First Continental Congress met in Philadelphia in September

1774. Every delegate agreed that American rights were being violated by British policies. At its second session, in fact, Congress unanimously resolved to publish a statement demonstrating which liberties were abridged. No unanimity existed, however, as to the best means of opposing objectionable parliamentary acts. The more radical delegates believed that only policies of countercoercion would impress Britain, while the conservatives—among whom Galloway emerged as the dominant spokesman—counseled that Congress should once again petition for redress of grievances and seek revision of the imperial constitution.[41]

It was quickly apparent that a majority of delegates wished Congress to adopt economically coercive measures. In mid-September Congress endorsed the resolution of Suffolk County, Massachusetts, which condemned British policy and advocated the discontinuance of all trade with Great Britain, Ireland, and the British West Indies. On 27 September Congress agreed to prohibit the importation of British goods until the distasteful legislation was repealed. Galloway voted for both measures. The following day, as Congress prepared to consider a cessation of American exports to Britain, Galloway proposed the conservative alternative.[42]

Galloway's speech of 28 September was short. He presented only the "great out-lines" of a plan for imperial union. He told the delegates that he hoped Congress would agree to the scheme and make additional recommendations. His plan, he continued, reflected the fact that the colonies could not be represented adequately in Parliament. If his plan for redress was accepted by Congress and in London, the "whole Empire may be drawn together on any emergency, the interest of both countries advanced, and the rights and liberties of America secured." The plan was simple: Great Britain should create an American branch of Parliament, which would not only govern the American colonies, but in imperial affairs would have powers equal to the existing branches of Parliament. The new parliamentary body should consist of a "President General," appointed by the King, and a "grand Council," to be chosen by the colonial assemblies every three years. Except in time of war, the assent of both the American and the existing houses of Parliament would be required to enact imperial legislation.[43]

The plan was "warmly seconded" by John Jay and James Duane, conservative delegates from New York, and by Edward Rutledge of South Carolina. Rutledge thought it "almost a perfect Plan," while Duane believed that together with economic pressures applied to Britain, Galloway's plan would afford the "Relief of Boston and Mass." and secure a "lasting Accommodation with G. Britain." Nevertheless, after a full day of debate, the radicals mustered sufficient strength—six colonies against five—to send the plan to committee for additional study. On 22 October Congress rejected the scheme and expunged all reference to it from the official journal.

THE LOYALIST MIND

Of "all the difficulties in the way of effective and united action," John Adams sighed, "the most alarming" had been eliminated. The effective action of which Adams wrote was quickly forthcoming—Congress passed countercoercive measures curtailing American consumption of British goods and prohibiting colonial exports to the mother country.[44]

The evidence is far from conclusive that adoption of the Galloway plan would have produced serious imperial negotiations. Britain might have remained unwilling to make a substantive offer to recalcitrant colonists, but the plan could have provided the ministry with the face-saving measure it required to pursue serious negotiations. It is clear, however, that Congress had an alternative to mere acceptance or rejection of ministerial policy. It is also clear that Congress' rejection of the compromise alternative made the violent rupture in Anglo-American relations—dreaded even by the radical delegates—a virtual inevitability.[45]

For the most part historians have been critical of the role Galloway played at the First Continental Congress. His failure, according to one scholar, was due to philosophical weaknesses in his plan and to his disabling political liabilities and errors. The plan not only suffered from an "almost perverse narrowness of view," but his plea for a negotiated settlement should have been made contingent on the withdrawal of all British troops from Boston. Furthermore, the plan failed because of his "purely constitutional definition" of the quarrel, even though "Congress . . . was no constitutional convention, but an assembly of desperate urgency." A new study of the year prior to hostilities disagreed, concluding that Galloway correctly assumed that the "very meeting of an intercolonial congress was a step toward the realization" of a "revision of the imperial constitution"; however, Galloway's plan was "doomed" because "his objectives ran counter to those of an overwhelming majority of the delegates." Another scholar attributed the rejection of the plan to Galloway's inability to understand the true nature of the crisis. The dispute was "uncompromisable," and Galloway was "blind to reality" in thinking the empire could be preserved. He failed, it has been suggested, because his concept of the rights of Americans was no longer within the mainstream of colonial thought by 1774. He attempted to " 'deduce' colonial rights singlehandedly from arbitrarily chosen premises." His defeat has even been ascribed to his great erudition, which "progressively isolated" him from the "public discussion." His plan of union was "too sophisticated for popular consumption." Galloway's personality, according to some, was an additional hindrance. He has been characterized as a man of such "haughtiness" and arrogance that he "succeeded only in making the way easy for his enemies." A recent study concluded that Galloway was "arrogant, overbearing and hot tempered," and that while these "traits were serviceable" in provincial politics, they were a liability in a national congress. Galloway committed so many tactical errors at the Continental Congress, in the estimation of one historian, that "it is perhaps not too much to say that he was the chief instrument in bringing about his own defeat." He failed, for instance, to consort adequately with delegates of contrasting viewpoints, he misjudged the attitudes of most congressmen, and he "simply underestimated the momentum of the revolutionary movement."[46]

Much of the scholarly criticism of Galloway has merit. It is apparent that Galloway and his allies made numerous tactical errors. Several years later, in fact, Galloway acknowledged that he had acted unwisely. He had been far too candid, he admitted, whereas his opponents "left no art . . . unessayed to conceal their intentions." In the discussions held "out of doors," he had foolishly been "open and ingenuous" with those he could not trust. Afterwards, he even tacitly recognized that the radicals were better organized and were superior politicians. For instance, by circulating false allegations—such as the story that British vessels had bombarded Boston, a well-orchestrated but unfounded rumor which reached Philadelphia just as Congress was beginning its debate on the Suffolk Resolves—his opponents succeeded in winning the allegiance of the Philadelphia populace. The Philadelphia "mob . . . loosened the firmness of some of the loyalists," he ruefully acknowledged.[47]

Some of the scholarly criticism, however, has been unwarranted. That Galloway's failure should be attributed to objectionable personality traits, for instance, is extremely conjectural. Although enemies thought him a man of "Design and Cunning," friends lauded him as a "man of Integrity" and "sound Judgemt. & Probity, and above the affectation of Tinsel and Ornament." Perhaps he was haughty, but that trait neither prevented his rise to the pinnacle of power in Pennsylvania nor inhibited the designs of similarly afflicted radicals at the Continental Congress.[48]

In addition, there is little evidence that the delegates manifested the same objections to the Galloway plan as have so many historians. No delegate objected to Galloway's "single-handed" assessment of colonial rights, because most congressmen shared the Pennsylvanian's point of view. Many delegates must have agreed with John Jay that the Plan of Union did not require the colonists to "give up any one Liberty . . . or interfere with any one Right." In mid-October Congress unanimously resolved, in language similar to that used by Galloway in his 28 September speech, that the colonists had "never ceded . . . the rights, liberties, and immunities of free and natural-born subjects within the realm of England." The colonists, Congress added, "are entitled to the benefit of such of the English statutes as existed at the time of their colonization," chief among which "is a right in the people to participate in their legislative council." Galloway could not

THE LOYALIST MIND

have objected to the contention of the Declaration of Rights that Parliament should regulate colonial trade in order to secure "the commercial advantage of the whole empire," that the colonists possessed the right to petition for redress of grievances, or that British laws should be applied equally throughout the empire. Galloway was clearly in agreement with the resolution which maintained that the rights of colonists were violated when taxes were levied "without their consent." Disagreement between Galloway and a majority of the delegates existed only over the proper means for securing the rights of the colonists. Even so, however, Galloway voted for a trade embargo—certainly for tactical, not philosophical reasons—the day before he formally presented his plan.[49]

Why, then, did the Galloway compromise plan fail? Certainly, a few radical delegates believed the Anglo-American quarrel was "uncompromisable." Great Britain had become so despicable in the eyes of some radical congressmen that the very idea of compromise—even if the ministry agreed to an American-offered plan—was viewed with abhorrence. Some openly hoped for a "Collision of british Flint and American Steel." Patrick Henry admitted that he preferred war to any compromise which failed to "liberate our Constituents from a . . . Nation [where] Bribery is a Part of her System of Government." Other congressmen were disillusioned by the repeated rejection of colonial supplications; still others despaired at the absence of any discernible sign of accommodation from London. Moreover, as some historians have argued recently, events by 1774 had prepared many congressmen "emotionally and intellectually" for "withdrawal from the empire" should Britain refuse to agree to the colonists' demands. By the time Congress met, furthermore, the growth of republican sentiment—and Galloway assuredly was not a republican—might have convinced some delegates that an imperial revolution was necessary for a "firmer establishment of basic rights . . . not only [for] America, but [for] Britain, too."[50]

Nevertheless, the majority in Congress hoped the quarrel might be peaceably resolved and that America's colonial status might be preserved. John Adams thought the "Commencement of Hostilities is exceedingly dreaded here" by delegates who "shudder at the prospect of blood." "Their opinions," he added, "are fixed against hostilities and rupture, except they should become absolutely necessary; and this necessity they do not yet see. They dread the thought of an action; because . . . it would render all hopes of a reconciliation with Great Britain desperate." Samuel Chase of Maryland expressed the majority sentiment when he stated that "Force . . . is out of the Question." Christopher Gadsden concurred. "I am for being ready," the South Carolinian asserted, "but I am not for the sword."[51]

Despite the hope that hostilities might be avoided, most delegates believed that any proposal for compromise which came from the colonies would be interpreted in London as a sign of American weakness or vacillation. A popular toast among congressmen prescribed "Wisdom to Britain, and Firmness to the Colonies." Samuel Adams noted that the delegates "strongly recommend[ed] perserverance in a firm and temperate conduct." Dickinson, who was added to the Pennsylvania delegation in October, thought the colonists were compelled to take "such grounds that Great Britain must relax, or inevitably involve herself in a civil war." Galloway, however, had not fully made the transition from peaceful protest to the use of countercoercive measures. He was, according to John Adams, "like the Tribe" in Massachusetts which had followed Governor Thomas Hutchinson. Galloway was "now just where the Hutchinsonian Faction were" in 1765, "when We were endeavoring to obtain a Repeal of the Stamp Act."[52]

Furthermore, if the Galloway plan did not require the relinquishment of colonial rights, it nevertheless constituted a threat to the powers of the provincial assemblies. Under his plan, the assemblies would have been subordinate to the new American congress. The scheme, Patrick Henry charged, would strip the colonies of hard-earned legislative prerogatives and "throw them into the arms of an American Legislature" likely to become as corrupt as the British model. Richard Henry Lee feared the "Plan would make such Changes in the Legislature of the Colonies" that the powers of the assemblies would be negated.[53]

Galloway's radical adversaries, moreover, believed they fully understood the Pennsylvanian and were aware of more than just the "out-lines" of his philosophy. He was, they believed, a Tory. John Adams thought Galloway a master of "Machiavilian Dissimulation" who only pretended "to be a stanch Friend to Liberty." Adams also believed Galloway had "accepted a seat in this Congress rather for the purpose of 'sitting on the skirts of the American advocates,' than of promoting any valuable end." Patrick Henry had a "horrid Opinion" of Galloway and was "very impatient to . . . not be at Liberty" to describe his "true Colours." It would not have been difficult for other congressmen to learn of Galloway's sentiments. As an important political leader for nearly twenty years, his positions on many issues were public knowledge. Presumably, information that was not publicly available was revealed "out of doors" by Galloway's Pennsylvania enemies—men like Dickinson, Charles Thomson, and Thomas Mifflin—with whom the radicals quickly allied as substantive issues came before Congress. The best of plans offered by a man with the reputation of being an unequivocal British sympathizer would have faced considerable opposition. "A Tory here," John Adams noted, "is the most despicable animal in the creation. Spiders, toads, snakes are their only proper emblems." Even Galloway's offer of the Pennsylvania State House as a meeting site was rejected. It was perhaps the most suitable location, "but as *he* offers, the other party oppose."[54]

In addition, some in Congress, alarmed at the nearly incessant imperial warfare, may have believed the Galloway plan would inevitably involve the colonists in undesired foreign wars. Galloway's scheme not only offered no safeguard against involvement in foreign conflicts, but it would have extended nearly dictatorial powers to Britain during time of war. Despite his earlier pledge to support any plan Galloway proposed, Franklin informed his partner that he could not endorse the compromise scheme because "I . . . apprehend more mischief than benefit from a closer union" with Great Britain. That "old rotten state," he feared, would "drag us after them in all the plundering wars which their desperate circumstances, injustice and rapacity may prompt them to undertake."[55]

Many congressmen undoubtedly believed rapid, positive colonial action was imperative. They feared that a prolongation of the dispute would so divide the colonists that redress would be unattainable. The extended stalemate which occurred during the Townshend Duties confrontation demonstrated that the colonial resolve was susceptible to collapse in a long test of wills. In that earlier crisis the colonists' economic boycott was beginning to unravel just at the moment Britain decided to repeal the duties. Furthermore, it was feared that if the dispute was not speedily resolved Great Britain might indict the congressmen for treason. In that eventuality the colonial assemblies might be intimidated and capitulate to Britain's demands. Other delegates were alarmed at the prospect of a prolonged period during which no legitimate government was discernible. "We want not only Redress, but speedy Redress," Thomas Lynch asserted. Anxiety at the course the restless multitude might take made Lynch blanch at the prospect of a society living without an established government for a long period.[56]

Galloway fought back against the congressional attacks on his plan. To those who argued that the Continental Congress was powerless to suggest constitutional reform, he answered that the delegates could recommend changes to the assemblies. They could then inform the imperial authorities of America's desires. To those who argued that the American branch would be corrupted, Galloway suggested that American virtue was sufficient to maintain American liberty. Moreover, the members of the Grand Council would be elected triennially. Most enlightened contemporaries agreed, he alleged, that if Parliament was elected every three years English corruption would be destroyed. Indeed, Congress could make the election of the American branch duennial or annual if it so desired. He denied the allegation that his plan would strip the colonial assemblies of their cherished powers. Legally, he insisted, the assemblies had no jurisdiction beyond limited police powers; his plan did not abridge those powers. Galloway maintained that the reforms he sought would give each assembly "a new jurisdiction, to decide upon regulations which relate to the general police of all the colonies."[57]

Nevertheless, since the vast majority of delegates were appalled at the thought of military coercion—and since the Galloway scheme promised only lengthy negotiations with no guarantee of success—Congress decided that the only alternative was for America to use its economy as an arsenal against the parent state. An American boycott of British goods "must produce a national Bankruptcy [in Britain] in a very short Space of Time," Samuel Chase argued. Lynch agreed that Parliament would be compelled to grant the colonists "immediate Relief. Bankruptcy would be the Consequence if they did not." Economic coercion "would come upon them like a Thunder Clap," Colonel Eliphalet Dyer predicted. Richard Henry Lee even maintained that the "same ship which carried home" the news of an American embargo "will bring back the Redress."[58]

Following the adjournment of Congress late in October, Galloway despondently returned to Trevose. His failure, he knew, probably terminated his career as a formidable power in Pennsylvania. The failure to resolve the crisis, moreover, increased the likelihood of imminent armed conflict between the colonies and the parent state. Although he had sunk into a state of depressive lethargy in the wake of previous failures, Galloway now became feverishly active. He fired off letters to allies in an effort to rekindle interest in his compromise scheme. He traveled to New Jersey and New York where he met secretly with Governors William Franklin and Cadwallader Colden. Early in 1775 he permitted a friend to publish the compromise scheme he had presented in Congress, then he too published the document. Later he publicly excoriated the colonial radicals. These actions violated the pledge each delegate had taken to maintain the secrecy of congressional deliberations; they also rendered obsolete the assumption of colonial unanimity.[59]

Galloway portrayed the popular leaders as scurrilous sorts, possessed of minds "fraught with dark and sinister designs." The "wretches" were the architects of "artful meanders and sophisticated labyrinths," of "unintelligible jargon and horrid nonsense." Under the influence of these "restless spirits," Galloway warned, America was preparing for war. The Continental Congress, the captive of this faction, had produced only that "ill-shapen, diminutive brat, INDEPENDENCY." America was poised on the brink of "the blackest rebellion, and all the horrors of an unnatural civil war." The real scheme of the radical leadership, he prophesied, was the establishment of republican government in America.[60]

The radicals, Galloway continued, were attempting to delude the colonists. Independence "could not meet with the approbation and support of the colonists . . . unless in some measure disguised; [thus] they have endeavored to throw a veil over it." This fraudulent tactic was "common to wrong-headed politicians who have not reason and truth to support their pretensions." Inglorious causes must always "be supported by sophisms, bold assertions, or evident untruths" while the "fair cause of liberty requires no such aids."[61]

A revolution, he argued, would have catastrophic results for America. In addition to the scourge of the British armed forces, the colonists would experience tyrannical rule at the hands of the popular party.[62] Even before a shot was fired Galloway cried that

> we see freedom of speech suppressed, the liberty and secrecy of the press destroyed, the voice of truth silenced; a lawless power [is] instituted throughout the colonies, forming laws for the government of their conduct, depriving men of their natural rights, and inflicting penalties more severe than death itself, upon a disobedience to their edict.[63]

Moreover, he predicted, economic debilitation would accompany the conflict. Commerce would stagnate, and agriculture would languish.[64]

Should the colonists attain independence from Britain—a most unlikely possibility, he thought—America's woes would have just begun. Foreign powers would seek to conquer the powerless new nation-state. The gravest threats would come from France and Spain, countries whose ambitions were active. A danger also existed that several nations might conspire to partition America. "The practice of conquering and dividing territories and kingdoms, is becoming fashionable in Europe," he warned, perhaps with an eye on recent occurrences in Poland. Galloway, however, really expected that the revolt must inevitably fail; then a full-fledged British occupation would result. Once defeated, the Americans would exchange their privileged status as English citizens for that of a "conquered people, subject to such laws as the conquerors shall think proper to impose."[65]

Galloway urged the colonists to desert the radicals. Were the colonists, he asked, still resolved

> to hazard all these direful misfortunes, rather than be united with your brethren and fellow subjects in Britain? If such be your dreadful resolutions, I, who have all that I hold dear and valuable among you, must content myself with sharing along with you the calamitous consequences of your frenzy, and the miserable fate of an American; with this only consolation, that I have honestly discharged my duty in warning you of your dangers; and endeavoured to pilot you into the haven of security and happiness.[66]

After the rejection of his compromise plan, Galloway might have attempted to prevent hostilities by means other than shrill pamphleteering. Despite his removal as Speaker of the Assembly in October 1774—an indication of the shift of opinion in Pennsylvania and of the deterioration of his influence—Galloway was not without power. He remained a member of the legislature and was selected to be a delegate to the Second Continental Congress. But Galloway decided that his compromise scheme would be no more attractive to the Second Congress than it had been to its predecessor. He opted, therefore, for the propaganda bombast of early 1775.

The propaganda campaign was accompanied by a last-ditch attempt to wring a condemnation of the radicals from the Pennsylvania Assembly. That plan collapsed as surely as his other schemes. Clutching at any straw which might prevent hostilities, Galloway and Governor Penn once again joined forces. The two urged the Assembly to pass a resolution condemning the proposed Second Congress and they sought to bypass Congress through an Assembly petition to the crown begging redress. Galloway launched his campaign with little support, but by mustering all his remaining powers of persuasion made the vote respectably close. Nevertheless, the motion was defeated by a vote of fifteen to twenty-two. In the course of the encounter, Galloway's life was threatened and his character was subjected to another blistering attack. Two months later, just as news trickled into Philadelphia of the bloodletting at Lexington and Concord, Galloway conducted his final legislative foray. He and Penn unsuccessfully urged the Assembly to endorse the House of Commons peace proposal of February 1775, a proposal which would have left no doubt as to the sovereignty of Parliament. Defeated and disillusioned, and with the city in the grip of war hysteria, Galloway resigned from both the Pennsylvania Assembly and the Continental Congress and retired to Trevose.[67]

Galloway's intention in withdrawing to Bucks County was not immediately clear, and it is unlikely that even he was certain of his ultimate course of action. Perhaps his penchant for inaction following a major defeat had reemerged. More likely, retirement seemed the most appropriate path for one who found Congress' means of opposing Britain unpalatable. His inability, moreover, to lead the Assembly in its moment of greatest crisis had been a staggering personal blow. Not even Franklin, who had returned from London in May, could activate Galloway. The old warrior made three arduous journeys to Trevose to urge Galloway to support the rebellion, but the younger partner rejected the entreaties. The two "parted as they met," Galloway later reminisced, "unconverted to the principles of each other."[68]

Galloway was probably uncertain of what role he would henceforth play in the imperial crisis. At times he seemed inclined to "content myself with sharing . . . the calamitous consequences" of the rebellion "and the miserable fate of an American." At other times he appeared to be "unalterably fixt in his duty to his sovereign . . . [and] determined to abide the consequences [of loyalism], however disastrous they might prove to himself and his family." He probably intended to watch events closely and act accordingly. But Galloway's philosophy would, as always, be his primary lodestar.[69]

THE LOYALIST MIND

2

Galloway and the War:
"A Zealous Loyalist"

While Galloway remained passive at Trevose, America was swept by turbulent events. Galloway waited and watched, unsure of what action to take—if, indeed, he was to act at all.

The tug of loyalty to his native country was great. Many of his friends, as well as most members of the political faction he had dominated, unhesitatingly joined the struggle against the parent state. Furthermore, Galloway had acknowledged the logic of certain of the American grievances against Britain, and during the initial year of hostilities the American leadership refrained from an actual declaration of independence. The struggle, the popular leaders insisted, was not a rebellion, not a separatist movement, but a battle to secure greater American autonomy within the empire.

Nevertheless, Galloway was drawn to the King. While he publicly indicated that the colonists had been denied their fair share of English liberties, the only manner of protest he recognized as legitimate was the submission of peaceful petitions to the crown. Philosophically he was impelled to support Great Britain. He had long been an imperial nationalist, and he was troubled by the American slurs against the British character. The colonial criticisms implied that some malignancy was gnawing at the empire from within the British constitutional system he so admired. Moreover, the prospects for a glorious American future, he believed, hinged on the continued paternalism of Great Britain.

It is unlikely that Galloway ever seriously harbored thoughts of supporting the colonists in their war against Great Britain. Such an act would have required a transformation totally out of character with the ideology he held from the beginning to the end of the Anglo-American upheaval. He cautiously observed the turmoil surrounding him, probably certain that he could never bring himself to support the rebellion, but otherwise unsure of his eventual deportment. His choice was between neutrality—if the colonial leadership would permit such an alternative—and allegiance to the crown.

During its first year the war must have seemed a riddle to Galloway, an isolated, retired politician living in rural Pennsylvania. The colonists scored some propaganda triumphs. The battles at Lexington, Concord, and Bunker Hill, as well as several indecisive engagements, were skillfully handled by American publicists. The colonists managed to put an army in the field while Britain, after an eight-year occupation, withdrew its troops from Boston. At the end of the year, in fact, the rebels held the thirteen insurgent colonies.

On the other hand, the colonists were not without difficulties. During that first year of war America suffered a spectacular defeat by its incapacity to seize Canada and its inability to lure those new British colonists into the contest against the parent state. There were other alarming portents for the rebels: no open foreign assistance was secured; the colonists remained far from united; thousands of Americans proclaimed their loyalty to Britain. Fissures existed even within the colonial leadership. The more radical leaders had gradually come to see reconciliation as unlikely, and they hoped to move America toward a proclamation of independence. Such a shift in policy, they believed, would assist in the procurement of badly needed foreign aid. More conservatively inclined leaders—men like Dickinson—were willing to use force against Britain, but shrank from the idea of separation. Importantly, too, the imperial authorities stood firm during the initial year of war. In August 1775 King George proclaimed that America was engaged in open rebellion; and, simultaneously, Britain arranged to hire foreign troops and agreed to send an army of 20,000 men to the colonies within a year. In November 1775 the ministry rammed the Prohibitory Act through Parliament. This measure, which some ministers openly called a "declaration of war" on the colonists, sought to quash all American commerce until the rebellion ceased.[1]

The character of the war changed markedly during its second year. A British army under Sir William Howe launched the first imperial offensive in the spring of 1776. New York was captured by September, and the colonial army under General George Washington narrowly succeeded in escaping to New Jersey. By autumn Howe had invaded that colony, too, and was marching rapidly south toward Philadelphia.

Meanwhile, America had undergone dramatic changes. The separatist movement grew steadily during the first year of hostilities and culminated in a congressional proclamation of independence in July. Galloway remained silent during the independence debate, although Philadelphia newspapers were filled with separatist essays and conservative counterattacks. Following independence, the authorities in Pennsylvania stepped up their campaign against the loyalists. Conditions for those suspected of Tory sentiments had steadily deteriorated since the commencement of hostilities. In June 1775, at the behest of Franklin, Philadelphia established a Committee of Safety to control its domestic enemies. Outlying villages soon followed suit. Avowed Tories were arrested; suspected persons were often harassed and intimidated, and some were jailed. After independence was proclaimed, the authorities instituted a campaign to decide whether these suspects were loyal to the new state of Pennsylvania. Furthermore, all acknowledged Tories and most moderates, including Galloway, were disfranchised when Pennsylvania elected a constitutional convention on 8 July. The convention chose Franklin as its president, and in September it reported the most democratic constitution approved during the Revolution— all property qualifications for voting and officeholding were removed; Pennsylvania was to be governed by a unicameral assembly; there was no provision for an executive official. On 5 November 1776 the state conducted its first elections under the new charter. Although the moderates, or anti-constitutionalists, mustered surprising strength in the Philadelphia area, the radicals were easily triumphant elsewhere.[2]

Three weeks after the Pennsylvania elections, Galloway at last acted. He packed what belongings he could gather into a wagon and set out for General Howe's encampment at New Brunswick, New Jersey. He was accompanied by several British sympathizers from his neighborhood. His wife, hoping to protect the family property, remained at Trevose.[3]

Several considerations moved Galloway to act. He may have been prompted by the increasingly portentous conditions in Pennsylvania. He deplored the sharply democratic features of the new constitution and the subsequent control of the state by its most radical elements. But his timing, at least to contemporaries and to more than a few historians, smacked of opportunism. The war had taken an ominous turn for America, and many thought that the rebellion would soon collapse. The survival of the American army—defeated, in retreat, a bitter winter just ahead—seemed remote. Moreover, as Howe swept into New Jersey he offered a proclamation of amnesty to all who were willing to swear an oath of loyalty to the King. With defeat apparently imminent, approximately 3,000 colonists eventually took advantage of this adroit gesture. While Galloway's actions may have had opportunistic overtones, he was probably unaware of the possibility of amnesty when he acted. Washington, with his intelligence apparatus, did not learn of the offer until 6 December, nearly two weeks after Galloway joined Howe.[4]

Galloway may well have joined the British forces out of fear. He later claimed he had fled to the asylum provided by General Howe because bands of marauding Whigs skulked about his estate. An excessive apprehensiveness had characterized his career; in fact, he frequently betrayed the classical symptoms of paranoia. His behavior reflected a recurring, exaggerated fear for his personal safety, as well as a preoccupation with the notion that conspiracies existed all about him. Between 1770 and 1773, while at his rural estate, he managed to convince himself that someone had attempted to extort money from him; that someone—he suspected Goddard, his former editor—was plotting his assassination; and that his daughter had conspired with some local knave to elope without his consent. Furthermore, although no delegate to the First Continental Congress was ever directly intimidated, Galloway later admitted that fear of the mob compelled him to vote for the colonial economic boycott. During the emotional Assembly debates in 1775, a foe, who perhaps understood Galloway's fearfulness, anonymously mailed a rope and halter to the assemblyman. The thinly veiled threat did the trick—Galloway almost immediately retired from Pennsylvania politics. His essays brimmed with accounts of real or fancied cabals. He depicted the uprising against Britain as the fruit of a conspiracy between Presbyterians and propertyless farmers. Still later he alleged that the British war effort was sabotaged by a traitorous element in London and by generals who were secretly attached to the republican principles of the rebellion which they had been assigned to crush. From the beginning of the imperial crisis until well after the war ended in 1783, Galloway insisted that America was jeopardized by conspiring foreign enemies and was too weak to stand unaided.[5]

It is not difficult to believe that Galloway, easily moved by exaggerated fears, was highly agitated during the summer and autumn months of 1776. When Pennsylvania authorities pledged to apprehend all suspected loyalists, Galloway grew frightened. In the fall of 1776, he went into hiding in New Jersey, and at times, out of fear, he posed as a champion of the rebellion. During the emotional fervor in 1776, for instance, he presented medals to an American militia regiment; on another occasion he entertained 400 colonial troops. His fears, however, were probably completely fabricated. At least Franklin, on the eve of his French mission in October 1776, was so unconcerned for the security of Trevose and the well-being of Galloway that he stored many years of treasured personal paper and correspondence at the estate for safekeeping. Whether or not Galloway's personal safety was imperiled in 1776, he was very much in character to have fancied the probability of injury at the hands of the popular party.[6]

THE LOYALIST MIND

Finally, his choice of allegiance reflected the philosophy he had held and championed since before imperial relations soured: he acted as an imperial nationalist seeking to reassert his revered British citizenship. Only the empire, he thought, could assure the security required by America. And the imperial reforms he desired would be made, if at all, only in the event that Great Britain crushed the rebellion. His outlook did not compel him to act. But if he chose to act, his philosophy dictated that he act in defense of the empire.

When Galloway openly proclaimed his loyalist sentiments, the end of the war seemed at hand. General Washington's army had steadily reeled from New York through New Jersey. Two weeks after Galloway reached the British encampment, Washington retreated into Pennsylvania amidst the first snowflakes of winter. Then the British suddenly encountered reverses. Washington daringly swept across the frozen Delaware River on Christmas night; his surprise operation startled the German mercenaries left in control of Trenton. Nearly 500 Hessians fled, but Washington, with a loss of only four slightly wounded Americans, seized almost a thousand of the enemy. The two armies parried for another week until, early in January, Washington routed a British force at Princeton. At the same moment that Galloway learned of these reversals, news trickled south that Britain's projected invasion of New York from Canada had failed. General Guy Carleton had inexplicably pulled back and canceled the assault upon meeting American resistance.

Although the rebellion continued, Howe was confident that 1777 would produce the final campaigns of the war. An intricate British strategy emerged from the winter planning sessions. General John Burgoyne was to lead a thrust from Canada into the heart of New York. Howe, meanwhile, was to sail from New York to Philadelphia; he expected to land about fifty miles southeast of the American capital at approximately the same moment Burgoyne seized Albany. The campaign proved to be a British disaster which opened the door for a Franco-American alliance. Burgoyne never reached his destination. He permitted his troops to be surrounded at Saratoga, where he surrendered a force of nearly 5,000 men to General Horatio Gates. Howe had better luck, although he failed to secure any significant victories. His weary troops landed in the Delaware Valley after a hot, sickening voyage of more than a month. They struggled toward Philadelphia, inconclusively contesting Washington along the way at Brandywine Creek. When Washington refused to make a stand in front of the capital, Howe entered Philadelphia on 26 September.

Galloway lived in close proximity to the British high command in America from the time he joined General Howe's army until Britain abandoned Philadelphia eighteen months later. He joined General Howe in New

York in December 1776 and remained in that city for more than six months. In June he accompanied Howe on a three-week expedition to New Jersey. He sailed on the *Alert Schooner* with Howe's Pennsylvania invasion fleet on 19 July 1776. During this entire period he acted as an intelligence officer, divulging what information he could about American plans, man-power, and geography. Galloway, who was in the field only during the period of Howe's march from Chesapeake Bay to Philadelphia, based his reports largely on information from the numerous agents with whom he had established contact. After the invasion of Pennsylvania he worked feverishly to create an information network both in Philadelphia and in the interior of Pennsylvania. His efforts won the grudging admiration of his adversaries and, additionally, led General Charles Cornwallis to characterize the infor-mation he provided as "very material" to the British war effort. Galloway helped secure provisions for the British armed forces, and he was even consulted in the preparation of military plans and operations.[7]

Although Galloway posed as an expert on the number of American loyalists, his inconsistent and erroneous reports on this subject helped foster the delusion in London that the rebellion was unpopular among the vast majority of colonists. In January 1778 he advised British authorities that five-sixths of the colonists remained loyal. Six months later he reported that nine-tenths of the population was loyalist. On several occasions he suggested that approximately eighty per cent of the colonists were loyal, while at another time he insisted that two-thirds of the American population sup-ported the British war effort. Sometimes he vaguely alluded to the "tens of thousands" who longed for the suppression of the rebellion. He declared that in some states fewer than one in every 150 inhabitants had supported the revolutionary state constitutions.[8]

Galloway never wavered in his belief that the number of loyalists steadily increased. Before the fighting began he predicted that the violence of radical protests would cause most colonists—even those who sympa-thized with the protestors—to desert the agitators. In early 1775, before Lexington and Concord, he wrote that a majority of colonists had finally seen that continued dissent would ultimately lead to independence and that radicalism would be rejected in order to prevent war. Even the military disaster at Saratoga in 1777 did not alter the optimistic tone of his reports. A few weeks after the battle he reported that the vast majority in America still desired the restoration of the empire. The cruelty of the Continental Army had convinced many of the undesirability of continuing the rebellion, he advised London. Other colonists, he said, had been converted to loyalism because of colonial currency depreciation, indebtedness, and heavy taxes, still others because of the personal inconvenience caused by war.[9]

Galloway also supplied intelligence regarding American troop

THE LOYALIST MIND

strength, although, as in the reports on loyalist numbers, his estimates varied. A few weeks after Saratoga he reported to a British adjutant that Washington had approximately 10,000 troops under his command. At the same time he advised the ministry that Washington's force numbered 12,000. One month later he reported that Washington's strength had declined to 6,000 men. Early in March he calculated that the American army had dwindled to 5,000, and later that month—and again in June—he observed that Washington had just 4,000 soldiers.[10]

Galloway's reports, in addition, stressed the difficulties which confronted the Americans. Approximately 2,500 of Washington's army died in the bitter winter of 1776–1777, he confided. He reported in 1777 that thirty to forty colonists were dying daily of starvation or illness in rebel-controlled Philadelphia. Before Howe commenced operations in 1778, Galloway reported that all of Washington's horses had perished at Valley Forge, and the troops were ill, without medicine, short of adequate supplies of food or clothing, and confined to "very uncomfortable Lodgings."[11]

Galloway predicted that suffering would eradicate the American army before the spring of 1778. Recruits could be obtained only on threat of fine, imprisonment, or execution. He claimed that entire counties, desperate to avoid serving, resisted induction; it was not uncommon for farmers to oppose recruiting officers with pitchforks and clubs. Desertion, he thought, further complicated Washington's problems. Galloway advised that nearly 1,500 Americans had deserted to Philadelphia by March of 1778. Later, when Britain occupied Philadelphia, he reported that Washington was confronted with nearly fifty desertions every day.[12]

Moreover, Galloway maintained, Washington's army was woefully unprepared to challenge the highly polished British troops. An army's quality, he once reflected, was more often determined by the character of its officers than by the number of its men. Whereas British officers were capable professionals and the enlisted men were well-disciplined veterans, the American officers were inexperienced and "badly appointed," and the "panic-stricken" troops were better suited for the "mechanic arts or the plow." In addition, Britain's superior soldiers were assisted by what Galloway thought was a first-rate intelligence network, while the colonists muddled along with a primitive apparatus. Late in the war Galloway told a British audience that Washington's intelligence service was so poor that the American commander frequently presumed he was in enemy territory when he was, in fact, on safe terrain. In Galloway's view, Washington was often poorly equipped—either the limited number of manufacturing concerns could not fulfill Washington's needs, or his supplies were destroyed by loyalist saboteurs. The British, furthermore, were attended by able surgeons and physicians while the colonists experienced untold suffering. His reports were filled with accounts of maladies which occurred in the after-math of battles. Finally, the recurrent desolation caused by both armies led Galloway to predict a famine for the colonists.[13]

Galloway scoffed at Congress' estimate of American manpower. The population of the colonies, he calculated, was 2,430,678, not 3,000,000 as claimed by Congress. Moreover, when allowances were made for the large number of slaves, free Negroes, women, children, and loyalists, the rebels could draw on fewer than 150,000 men capable of soldiering. Some of these were unhealthy—many had previously been wounded—and others were needed on the home front for economic reasons or to guard against slave insurrections. The "Strength of America must be . . . nearly exhausted," he reported in 1778.[14]

The intelligence reports filed by Galloway were not always accurate. Some errors inevitably arose from the very nature of intelligence gathering, but other miscalculations were due to his overweening desire to retain Britain's interest in the war. Galloway's reports, therefore, grew less reliable as he became increasingly disillusioned with the course of the war. His early reports on the strength of the insurrectionaries were reasonably precise. Although he erred slightly in reporting too few troops under Washington early in 1778, he overestimated the number of troops under the American commander at Valley Forge. When the popularity of the war decreased in Britain, Galloway's reports adjusted to that fact. He maintained in 1779 that Washington's forces had declined to 4,000, when, in fact, the American general commanded nearly 11,000 soldiers and hoped to have 25,000 men under arms before the end of that summer.[15]

Although he exaggerated Washington's recruitment problems, Galloway's reports on the difficulties confronting the Americans during the winters of 1776–1777 and 1777–1778 were substantially correct. Washington estimated that 1,100 men deserted or refused to reenlist in early 1777, and he wondered "how we shall be able to rub along till the new army is raised." The following winter the American commander reported that 4,000 of his soldiers were "unfit for duty because they were bare foot and otherwise naked." Like Galloway, Washington reported that "unless some great and capital change suddenly takes place . . . this Army must inevitably be reduced to one or another of three things: Starve, dissolve or disperse." Furthermore, while Galloway underestimated the number of potential American soldiers, his estimate of the total colonial population was more accurate than the guess made by Congress. Recent scholarly studies placed the colonial population at 2,000,000 inhabitants in 1763 and at 2,500,000 in 1776, whereas Galloway estimated just over 2,400,000, and Congress thought 3,000,000 people lived in the colonies.[16]

The most serious error made by Galloway was in his continued assurance that large numbers of colonists remained loyal to Great Britain. His consistently inaccurate reports on this subject eventually led General Howe to conclude—although Howe did not acknowledge his feelings until much later when his relations with Galloway had soured—that the American was a "nugatory informer." Recent studies—which disclose that at most one-third of the colonists remained loyal—signify that he erred on the side of generosity. Even so, Galloway was accountable only for Pennsylvania, a state that contained an unusually high number of loyalists. Moreover, a recent study has indicated that the number of British sympathizers—never a stable and uniform aggregate—tended to increase markedly in regions where fighting occurred, and Galloway's reports were issued in the period when Pennsylvania was under siege.[17]

During the occupation of Philadelphia General Howe designated Galloway "Superintendent General of the Police in the City and its Environs & Superintendent of Imports and Exports to & from Philadelphia." He gathered a staff and proceeded to a multiplicity of duties. With Andrew Elliot, who held a similar post in New York, Galloway attempted to regulate the commerce of the Middle Atlantic region. He persisted in his intelligence activities around Philadelphia. He attempted to set prices to combat inflationary tendencies. He was at last permitted to oversee the recruitment of loyalist forces. Galloway personally raised a troop—he had asked permission to raise a regiment—and he later claimed to have recruited nearly 13,000 men during this brief period. Although not a police official in the strictest sense of the word, he directed the disarmament of those known to have supported the rebellion, and he was responsible for the maintenance of civil peace in occupied Philadelphia.[18]

The British occupation of Philadelphia was short-lived. When news of Burgoyne's disaster at Saratoga reached London, the ministry reassessed its strategy. Any lingering doubts as to the wisdom of change were dispelled when the government learned of a formal Franco-American alliance. War with France was now a certainty. Britain therefore decided to suspend its previous strategy of attempting to capture Washington's army; instead, Britain now planned to crush the rebellion through a naval blockade and an invasion of the southern colonies, a region which supposedly abounded with loyalist allies. The ministry also dispatched a commission to America with an offer for a negotiated settlement. In May the loyalists learned that Philadelphia was to be abandoned to General Washington. Howe crassly suggested that the loyalists stay on and attempt to make peace with the rebels. For a short time Galloway contemplated making an overture to Washington, perhaps believing that he could serve both sides as a mediator in the prolonged war. He finally decided to stay with the British. Like his friend Ambrose Serle, Howe's secretary, Galloway may have secretly realized that

"he could only be to them a ruined Enemy, & to us an inefficient Friend."
Moreover, General Henry Clinton, Howe's successor, rejected the plan to
permit the loyalists to seek amnesty from the Americans. Clinton realized
that if the Pennsylvania Tories were accorded amnesty at this critical time,
loyalists throughout America would appeal for similar treatment. Clinton
therefore provided transport to New York for the Pennsylvania loyalists.[19]

Until that moment Galloway had not been openly critical of British
strategy. Now he fired off a stern note to the ministry which castigated the
decision to abandon Philadelphia. He argued that the city's central location
and excellent harbor made it a place of vital importance to both Britain and
the colonists. The manufacturing establishments of the city were too valuable to be relinquished, while possession of the shipyards would enable the
rebels to construct their own fleet. The region around Philadelphia contained enough fertile land to provide food for Washington for years. Finally,
Galloway argued, British occupation of Philadelphia had a jolting psychological impact on America. As long as the city remained in British hands
the rebels were dispirited; prolonged occupation would convert many revolutionaries into loyalists. Only those inhabitants who had been "elevated
from Dunghill in their present Power and Wealth are determined to keep
the Bull to the last Extremity."[20]

When Philadelphia was evacuated in June 1778, Galloway and his
daughter Elizabeth accompanied the British to New York. That fall they
sailed for England. Admiral Howe offered them passage, but Galloway
pleaded that he would be detained by business in New York for a few more
days. He later made the voyage on a transport and arrived in London in
December.[21]

Grace Galloway remained behind once again to fight for retention of
the family's property. She struggled hopelessly. Within a year she was
compelled to move to a small apartment in a dingy portion of the city. She
longed to leave America and advised her daughter never to return to the
colonies. But she refused to abandon Philadelphia as long as hope existed
for a British victory. "I know all is lost," she admitted in her diary for the
first time in August 1779. Thereafter, she filled the diary with bitter passages vilifying her husband. He had not adequately cared for his family, she
lamented. She despised his "vanity & baseness"; she was "now truly set
against him." She raged at Galloway's "Ungenerous conduct," for he "hurt
me more than all the proventials . . . had done."[22]

Galloway was also bitter and frustrated by the time he landed in
England. He was alone in a strange country. He had moved to London out
of consideration for his personal safety and because he believed he could
play a significant role in altering Britain's conduct of the war. His fate now
would not only be decided across the sea on the battlefields of America, but

in the chambers of Parliament and the councils of the ministry. The decision to sail to England was probably dictated by his awareness that opposition to the American war had increased greatly in Britain since the disaster at Saratoga and the consummation of the Franco-American alliance.

There had, of course, been an anti-war faction in England since before the commencement of hostilities. In the early stages of the conflict this faction denigrated the war as unconstitutional and unnecessary. As the war dragged on and the threat of French intervention increased, many Britons began to depict the conflict as "national suicide." By 1778, for example, many influential merchants and country gentlemen sought to end the war. Most Englishmen, however, still wanted a compromise settlement which would preserve the empire, and on the heels of the crushing defeat at Saratoga the ministry made its final attempt at rapprochement. If the colonists were willing to drop their demand for independence, the North ministry was prepared to remove standing armies from the colonies during peacetime, to agree to never alter a colony's charter without the colony's consent, to aid the colonists in meeting their debts, to permit the establishment of an American bank, to permit colonists to elect all civil officers, to remove all crown officers deemed unnecessary by the colonists, to appoint colonists to the customs service, to permit the existence of an American congress, and to allow the colonists to raise revenue as they desired for the support of their own militia forces. In return the North administration expected that the colonists would submit exports to Europe for parliamentary taxation, that the colonists would permit British taxation of all non-British manufactured goods imported to America, and that the colonists would agree to restore all confiscated loyalist property to its proper owners. Although the offer met all the demands which the Continental Congress had made in 1774, it was no longer acceptable to the American leadership. The plan was rejected, and shortly thereafter France entered the conflict as an American ally.[23]

These events strengthened the position of Englishmen who regarded the colonies as less than essential to the British economic welfare. The leading exponent of such an ideology was Josiah Tucker, the Anglican Dean of Gloucester. Before the rebellion Tucker questioned the necessity for England to retain the colonies. He believed colonies were expensive nuisances which required constant nursing and warfare and which provided the mother country with few material benefits in return. He thought England could secure its raw materials from cheaper sources; moreover, English manufactured articles were so inexpensive they could dominate any market. The colonies, he estimated, cost England between £300,000 and £400,000 annually in commercial losses alone. This money, he asserted, could be put to better use in England. Furthermore, Tucker regarded colonial revolts as inevitable and colonial independence as an eventual certainty. Even when independent, however, he believed America would continue to seek commercial relationships with Great Britain, so that in the final analysis England would be as prosperous as before the rebellion and at the same time would be freed of imperial headaches. By 1776 Adam Smith had expressed similar sentiments. In his celebrated *Wealth of Nations*, Smith alluded to the colonists as a liability for the parent state. He believed the colonies to be an economic detriment to England. Colonialism, he charged, disrupted the "natural balance" between English industries and curtailed Britain's access to foreign markets. Smith advocated cutting America loose from the empire. If the two parted on friendly terms, he thought, Anglo-American trade would flourish as it had during the imperial years.[24]

Many Englishmen championed American independence because of a commitment to a libertarian political ideology. John Cartwright epitomized this school of thought. In his *American Independence and the Interest and Glory of Great Britain*, Cartwright rejected the concept of parliamentary sovereignty in the empire. He asserted that charters made by earlier generations could not bind later generations. America was, and should be, independent, and Britain should treat America as a "sister kingdom."[25]

Unable to negotiate an end to the war, the North administration faced an obvious dilemma by mid-1778. The government was confronted with the prospect of either continuing an increasingly unpopular war against the colonies while it battled France or conceding independence to America. Lord North was so perplexed that he sanctioned the publication of a pamphlet by Israel Maudit, an administration propagandist, which urged independence for the colonists. The harried North evidently hoped the essay would serve as a trial balloon to gauge public sentiment. Maudit argued that a British victory against America was impossible and that in such circumstances further bloodletting was unconscionable. In addition, he wrote, British militarism provoked so much calumny by the Americans that a free United States would never consider commerce with England. Consequently, Maudit recommended immediate independence in the hope that such a generous policy would restore American love for England.[26]

Whatever North's motivations, Maudit's pamphlet stirred a considerable debate in London. A steady stream of publications appeared, some condemning the war and advocating independence for America. By the end of 1778, for the first time since the beginning of hostilities, a sizable number of newspapers treated the war as lost. The ministry, of course, was not without its defenders. These writers not only depicted independence in the darkest terms but insisted that the rebellion could still be crushed.[27]

Upon his arrival in London Galloway became one of the most active and diligent of the loyalist exiles who attempted to prolong Britain's interest in the American war. He also worked feverishly to protect the economic interests of the unfortunates who had been banished from the colonies. Galloway frequently met with ministerial officials to implore their assistance, and he became active in the Loyalist Association, an agency formed by several influential expatriates in the spring of 1779. This refugees' federation petitioned various British officials, including the Monarch, and served generally as an organization which publicized the loyalist view of the origin and nature of the colonial rebellion. Primarily, however, Galloway served the loyalist interest as a writer; he produced thirteen pamphlets between the time he arrived in London and the end of the war five years later. Most of these polemics were hastily written in a desperate attempt to sustain British interest in the war. Galloway propounded four themes in these essays. He attempted to show that Britain's well-being depended on American participation in the empire; he castigated the manner in which the military had conducted the war; he proposed a strategy which he believed would ultimately crush the rebellion; and he tirelessly urged imperial reform along the lines of the plan he presented to the Continental Congress.[28]

Galloway vehemently attacked the arguments of Dean Tucker and Adam Smith. He insisted that it was fallacious to assume that loss of the American colonies would not be detrimental to Great Britain. Simple logic, he asserted, proved that an empire of 4,000,000 inhabitants would be stronger than an empire with half that population. Moreover, the economic stability of the empire would be weakened by independence—the mainland colonies constituted almost half of England's foreign trade. Nearly two-thirds of the remaining imperial trade was between Britain and the West Indies, and Galloway had no doubt that an independent America would ultimately seize control of those islands. In addition, total American exports doubled approximately every decade. By the eve of the rebellion America exported over £4,500,000 of goods to England, and by 1800 American commerce would probably exceed the total trade of England. Before the revolution, Galloway reminded the critics of the war, the American colonies purchased half of England's manufactured goods. America would continue to be an even more lucrative market for these items. American industrialization was not likely until the continent was filled and the cost of labor declined. It was foolhardy, he counseled, to expect the imperial trade to continue once the empire collapsed. Although it was true that the colonies and England shared a common culture, the prospect for trade between an independent America and Great Britain was slight. If America could obtain no commercial alliance with a continental power, or if Anglo-American enmity ceased, or—finally—if America failed to manufacture its own necessities, trade might flourish as before the rebellion. Galloway doubted, however, that any of these conditions would occur. He noted that the Americans had already established trade relations with continental powers during the wartime emergency. And, historically, bad feeling between former belligerents died slowly. Finally, an independent America would industrialize because it would "readily perceive that manufactures are the great foundation of commerce, that commerce is the great means of acquiring wealth, and that wealth is necessary to her own safety." American independence, Galloway charged, would also doom Britain's control of the Newfoundland fisheries and would trigger a cycle, beginning with the loss of nearly 30,000 fishing jobs, which would ultimately plunge Britain into economic chaos.[29]

The maintenance of the empire was, moreover, a military necessity for England, according to Galloway. It was fashionable to argue that America had been of little help in the colonial wars, but Galloway—a former exponent of that theory himself—now contended that America had played a leading role in the establishment of British hegemony in the New World. America's potential for power was phenomenal. The population, by natural increase alone, could be expected to double in the next quarter century; augmented by massive immigration, he warned, the American population would soon exceed that of England. American armed might, he predicted gloomily, would thereafter surpass British potency. As America's naval power rose—through her own potential strength, as well as through the likely continuation of her alliances with European nations—Britain's naval strength would diminish. The source of England's naval stores would vanish when America became independent. The fisheries would henceforth produce experienced seamen for the United States navy. Before the power of the New World armada, Galloway continued, not even India would be safe for Britain. Certainly England would become prey to continental powers, and she could not anticipate assistance from America. In an early statement of what was later called the doctrine of American isolationism, Galloway argued that the "prosperity or ruin of kingdoms, from whose power she can have nothing to fear, and whose assistance she can never want, will be matters of . . . indifference" to America. "She can wish for no other connection with Europe, than that of commerce," he added, "and this will be better secured in the hands of an ally."[30]

In short, those who would grant independence to America contended for

> nothing less than to dismember, from the British community, the *greatest part* of its territory, and more than one *fourth part* of its people, and to give up near *one half* of its commerce . . . which united, must necessarily involve the decay, if not the ruin, of the best sources of wealth and strength in the possession of the empire; more especially, as a great part of what we shall give up must fall into the hands of our natural and determined enemies.[31]

THE LOYALIST MIND

A united empire, Galloway exclaimed, promised an alluring future of expansion and aggrandizement. It was a maxim of international relations that "a nation which possessed the most extensive territory . . . must be the *richest* and most *powerful*, and consequently the safest" of countries. Eventually, he predicted, a united Anglo-America would "acquire universal dominion over all America," including the unsettled frontier and the "mines of gold and silver, in South America."[32]

Galloway also clashed sharply with those militarists who had conducted the war. Here he was on precarious ground. Political realities dictated that his bludgeoning attacks be concentrated only on the generals and admirals. No mention of ministerial culpability could be risked, for if the government collapsed it was likely to be replaced by an administration willing to recognize American independence. In fact, he claimed that "the exertions of the Ministry in preparing for the suppression of the Rebellion have been truly great and noble, and more than equal to the end."[33]

Before the war Galloway had argued that Great Britain could easily defeat America. The colonists, he contended as early as 1775, "may as well attempt to scale the moon, and wrench her from her orbit as withstand the powers of Britain." After 1778 his position changed, and he suggested that Britain was invincible so long as the conflict was properly waged. He was convinced that British strategy had been sound until mid-1778, but he believed the implementation of that strategy had been woeful. The prime reason for British failure was inept generalship. He maintained that the British commanders had been indolent. Galloway called the generals "wise-acres" and alleged that they were more inclined to merriment than embattlement. One could only conclude, he added, that the field commanders were either ignorant or cowardly.[34]

Galloway was baffled by the failure to execute well-conceived British plans. He congratulated General Howe on his repeated success in permitting the enemy to escape. During the terrible winter of 1777–1778, for example, Washington remained unmolested at Valley Forge, when a British blow might have ended the rebellion. In fact, Galloway added, Washington was not only untouched but was allowed to destroy British stores of food, to forage in the nearby countryside, and to terrorize the local loyalists. Galloway urged that an attack be made on Washington at Valley Forge. If Washington's "Army should ever be dispersed," he reported, "as it was twelve Months since, which I imagine it may well be by Vigorous and steady pursuit, I think . . . the Congress in the present State of their Affairs and in the present Disposition and Temper of the People, will not be able to raise another of any . . . Consequence." Attack and pursuit, he asserted, were vital components of strategy when fighting an army such as Washington commanded. Because America had no garrisons, the rebellion would be crushed only when the army was conquered. "Force, however great," he concluded, "is useless unless exerted, and victory is Vain unless pursued."[35]

If Galloway found their lack of vigor reprehensible, he was mortified at the results when the generals decided to fight. The debacle of 1777 was a case in point. When Howe moved his army from New York to Philadelphia, he made what Galloway regarded as an unnecessary 600-mile transit by sea—he sailed south to Chesapeake Bay and then north to the Maryland coast—when a relatively safe 60-mile overland route across New Jersey would have been satisfactory. Howe undertook the voyage during the hottest season of the year, an unfortunate decision since the resulting shortages of water debilitated the cargo of men and horses. Moreover, Howe was accompanied by 20,000 troops; General Burgoyne, who was invading New York from Canada at that moment, was left with an undermanned army to campaign in America's "most disaffected area." But Burgoyne was not beyond reproach. He might have saved his army, Galloway maintained, had he not unwisely diverted a portion of his troops into the ambush at Bennington on the eve of the battle at Saratoga. Burgoyne's defeat was merely "melancholy proof" of his military inadequacy.[36]

Once the British launched a campaign, Galloway complained, the commanders invariably divided their forces. One-third of the army, he charged, was always employed in desultory plundering expeditions, another third was wasted in fruitless marches, and the remainder was left inactive. Galloway concluded that the generals often frittered away precious time and manpower on inconsequential targets. General Clinton's occupation of Charleston in 1780 was an excellent example of this unfortunate practice. Galloway thought the city was at least 1,000 miles removed from the real center of the rebellion. Moreover, after taking Charleston, Clinton returned to New York to engage in "plundering expeditions, which always do no good, [and] much mischief." Meanwhile, General Cornwallis, with the remainder of Clinton's army, proceeded northward from South Carolina "as if he thought he had been hunting a fox." Cornwallis scoured 1,500 miles, yet he neither secured nor reduced the region he traversed.[37]

Most of Galloway's venom was directed against army commanders, but he sometimes lashed out at the navy. With its immense numerical superiority, as well as its advantages accruing from experience, Galloway was bewildered at what he regarded as the navy's minimal success. He believed that Britain's numerical advantages increased each year—by the end of 1777 Britain had nearly seventy more warships afloat than her adversaries. Furthermore, the English fleet consisted of larger, more heavily armed vessels. A fleet of the British magnitude, he calculated, could line the length of the American coast, yet the British blockade was largely a failure. Not only did America continue to import foreign goods, but the intercolonial coastal trade flourished as well. Washington's army at Valley Forge was saved from famine because it received salt and pork funneled north from the Carolinas. Galloway argued that Admiral Richard Howe required only half his fleet to establish a blockade sufficient to destroy an already ill-provisioned army. Since an effective blockade would have destroyed the colonial naval force, the insurgent population—dependent on foreign imports for most of its goods—would have been further demoralized. Furthermore, American ports were seldom properly fortified, yet Howe neither made serious raids nor utilized neighboring loyalists for the destruction of the colonial fleet. Just four British vessels, Galloway admonished the Admiral, would have demolished the American fleet before it sailed. Instead, the colonial vessels were saved by British incompetence and were ultimately armed with French cannon. These same American vessels, Galloway sardonically charged in 1779, were later employed with great success as privateers against Howe's fleet.[38]

The most serious accusation which Galloway made—and his least supportable allegation—was that the conduct of the British generals was treasonous. The leading officers, he charged, had allied with members of the opposition factions in British political life to accomplish their desired objectives. Both groups hoped to prolong the war until the ministry collapsed. This cabal, however, had more in mind than merely acquiring power. The plotters hoped to strip the monarch of his constitutional prerogative to appoint his own servants. Once this revolutionary plan was accomplished, Galloway said, the King would be compelled to place members of the opposition faction where "they may command the purses, and riot in the wealth of [their] fellow-citizens." The conspirators, realizing that the existing ministry would be removed only if its rule appeared incompetent, were prepared, if necessary, to contrive at the dismemberment of the empire in order to topple the King's ministers. To accomplish its ends, the cabal frequently incited London's mobs to riot and agitate against the war. General Howe, in Galloway's estimation, was the *agent provocateur* of the conspiracy. Galloway believed that Howe and Franklin had fostered the American insurrection. Howe, furthermore, had succeeded in prolonging the conflict by secretly transmitting British peace proposals to the Americans long before the plans were formally presented to colonial negotiators. Primed for the presentation of these plans, the colonists speedily rejected all offers. Howe, Galloway charged, cooperated with Franklin in drafting the American peace plans in such a manner that they were certain to be unacceptable to the ministry.[39]

Despite Great Britain's horrendous military plight after several years of warfare, Galloway remained confident that the rebellion could still be suppressed. History demonstrated, he insisted, that Britain customarily began its military campaigns in an inept fashion only to eventually overcome the foe. The most immediate change which Galloway recommended was an alteration in British strategy. The previous plan, he claimed, was not adequate for the reduction of a civil rebellion. A domestic upheaval would quickly collapse when confronted by "quick, sudden, rapid" measures; however, a government which was lax in subduing rebels was soon in difficulty. As rebellions were easily generated, they were easily crushed. "A little Success mixed with Enthusiasm," he asserted, "will induce Cowards to turn out."[40]

Galloway recommended that greater use be made of the Indian allies and that less reliance be placed on the Hessian mercenaries. He did not believe the Indians should commit acts of cruelty, but he did advocate using the natives on the frontier to destroy the farms which supplied the American army. Many Indians remained neutral in the struggle because of prior cavalier treatment at the hands of British officials. A wise Indian policy would have forestalled French intervention, he maintained, for the French would have been reluctant to combat their old allies. He regarded the German mercenaries as undependable troops, prone to desert when tantalized by the lure of American bounty. Galloway thought it a policy of "unparalleled absurdity" to garrison strategic bases with mercenaries as Howe had done at Trenton in 1776. In addition, German brutality often alienated potential colonial allies. The Hessians were often accused of unspeakable atrocities. With such friends the British would not be regarded as liberators, but as "OPPRESSORS AND PLUNDERERS."[41]

While in London, surrounded by exiled Tories, Galloway persisted in encouraging Britain to make greater use of the loyalists. He could not understand Britain's neglect. Unless Britain quickly made use of this fifth-column element, he admonished, their services might be permanently withheld. The loyalists, he predicted, were unlikely to assist the parent state once they had experienced the "tormenting sting of neglect." Nevertheless, as late as 1780 he maintained that the loyalty of the majority of colonists remained inviolate.[42]

Since many of the colonial elite remained true to Britain, Galloway recommended that they be used as sources of intelligence, as propagandists, and as commanding officers. His own success in quickly raising a loyalist force in occupied Philadelphia convinced him of the willingness of these people to serve. He recommended that some of them be used behind American lines as saboteurs; specifically, he argued that rebel ships in port could be destroyed, and he even concocted plans for the abduction of the Governor of New Jersey and—in a dramatic flight of fantasy—for the kidnapping of the entire Continental Congress. In addition, Galloway counseled Britain on the need for retaining the allegiance of large numbers of colonists if the empire was to be reconstructed.[43]

THE LOYALIST MIND

Galloway also urged the British command to throw off its affinity for the European manner of warfare. British armies routinely awaited summer weather before operations were launched, a policy which robbed Britain of several critical weeks of campaigning. Roads in America, he argued, were generally passable by early April; and, if the early spring weather was occasionally bad, these factors should have been more detrimental to an untrained militia than to a professional army. In addition, Washington's troops were normally at their weakest in early spring following a long, debilitating winter. Nevertheless, Galloway paradoxically denounced the argument—often voiced by the opponents of the war in Britain—that the assets of British military experience and numerical superiority were negated by the uniqueness of American conditions. He observed that America had no hedges or dikes. Its fences were wooden and certainly not insurmountable. He asked where were the hills on Long Island, or between New York and Trenton, or between Head of Elk and Philadelphia. Most battle areas had no mountains and the hills were little more than "mole-hills." If ambushes against Howe, Clinton, or Burgoyne were possible, they had also been tried—with little success—against Amherst, Forbes, and Bouquet. To Galloway the entire argument was a dodge. "I have no idea," he remarked, "of any country being impartial in respect to military operations."[44]

In the early days of the struggle Galloway hoped that Britain would be charitable toward its colonies, but as the war progressed he came to believe that new tactics were required. Britain's "low minded and relentless Enemies," he charged, did not deserve lenient treatment. Galloway scoffed at Burgoyne's assertion that although unsuccessful in battle, he had not resorted to terrorism. Undoubtedly mindful that his actions were dictated by political considerations, Burgoyne maintained that British officers were to act as soldiers, not as executioners. Galloway attacked these "romantic sentiments" and advised the General that the lofty ideals had "not paid the *texture of your* mind any great compliment." Terror was "a settled & established rule of conduct" for military men. If a general was unfamiliar with the uses of terror, he was to be pitied; but if a general was familiar with terrorism and shrank from its application, he deserved only contempt. Failure to utilize every means of warfare only caused the rebellion to be protracted. Galloway thought it virtually impossible to be overzealous in suppressing the revolution. Although he did not say precisely what he had in mind, Galloway charged that the military man must be a "soldier-executioner." If necessary, the British must annihilate the enemy's country, for it was preferable that America be destroyed than be "annexed to, & joined with France, in order to annihilate this Empire."[45]

Galloway, of course, urged sweeping changes in the military leadership. Moreover, he advised Britain to occupy all vital coastal cities and to institute a dynamic policy of searching out and destroying rebel armies. Armed loyalists, he added, could then secure the conquered areas. He perceived that British forces must become as mobile as the rebels. It was folly, he recognized, to refuse to engage or to half-heartedly pursue the colonial armies. The war would end only when rebel forces were crushed. Once Washington's troops were defeated the colonists and their French allies would lose interest in the contest.[46]

Finally, Galloway believed the government should propose enlightened imperial reforms. When reforms were implemented loyalist ranks would swell. Throughout the war he urged British leaders to reconsider his compromise scheme of 1774. He repeatedly recommended that Parliament sanction the establishment of an American congress, that Britain nullify all pre-1763 parliamentary acts, that the mercantilistic trade and currency restrictions be removed or at least relaxed, and that sweeping changes be instituted in the provincial governments in the occupied states. He advocated that all governors and councils be appointed by the crown and that the lower houses of assembly be elected by colonial property owners. If these alterations were made in the Anglo-American constitution, he prophesied, the civil war would end and the colonists would "adhere to the State, attend her faithfully, in all her wars and distresses, *fight her battles, and expire with her.*"[47]

Late in the war Galloway summarized his formula for victory:

> Let there be *a change of the measure for carrying on our internal military operations.* . . . Instead of suffering our vastly superior force to sleep in New-York during four campaigns, disgracefully besieged by an undisciplined and truly contemptible enemy, let it be *ordered into the field.* Instead of wasting our money . . . *let the army be ordered to proceed after the main force of the Congress, pursue and destroy it,* taking care to establish *peace and civil authority in the country as we conquer it.* Instead of robbing indiscriminately . . . *stop the rapine* and *disgraceful plunder of the officers and men, and convince the people, that our troops come as their DELIVERERS.* . . . Instead of rejecting the loyal force . . . *enjoin our Generals to embrace it with zeal* and cordiality.[48]

How should the strategy which Galloway had recommended since 1777 be assessed? There was little unanimity within the imperial command—or within the opposition factions—as to the proper strategy, and historians have long been at odds in their assessment of British policy. No definitive appraisal is likely. Nevertheless, it seems certain that much of the criticism by Galloway was unwarranted. For example, his suggestion that the American terrain and weather should have been no hindrance to British armies revealed a lack of military knowledge. Movement by a large army along muddy, rain-soaked roads was a near impossibility. The nature and

THE LOYALIST MIND

size of the continent often precluded prompt communication and concerted action among commanders. If, as Galloway suggested, British officers had succeeded on American soil in earlier wars, their major enemy had been other European—not native American—soldiers. In addition, Galloway regarded the southern strategy as foolish, yet the strategy was based largely on the assumption—fostered by loyalists—that thousands of southern Tories would rise to assist the English troops. Neither Galloway nor the generals he criticized fully appreciated the American forces. Part of the British failure was due to the effective campaigns waged by the Continental army. Washington demonstrated that a small force, when properly used, could harass and stalemate a larger, better-trained army. The American commander's actions further demonstrated that British numerical superiority, of which Galloway wrote at such length, was often ineffective against colonial hit-and-run warfare. In fact, the British forces were probably too small to achieve the ends desired by the administration.[49]

It is questionable, moreover, whether the strategy proposed by Galloway would have produced a colonial defeat or led to costly British victories similar to that at Bunker Hill. And his contention that Britain's attitude toward the Indians was supercilious was strangely ill informed. Great Britain sought and received considerable assistance from numerous tribes. Furthermore, many of his suggestions were contradictory. He recommended constant pursuit and battle, yet he criticized British generals for not leaving an occupation force in previously subdued territory. He called for a more ruthless British attitude, yet he charged that the pitiless actions of the Hessians resulted in colonial hatred.

Nevertheless, some of Galloway's criticism was valid. General Howe was extremely reluctant to fight Washington. In the winter Howe blamed the cold for his inaction; in the summer he argued it was too hot for combat. Howe often lacked the resources he desired, but he was always better equipped than his adversary. Galloway's criticism of Howe for beginning his campaigns too late and completing them too early was not unrealistic. Howe, for example, did not begin his 1777 offensive until late August, and he completed that campaign in early November. In Washington's estimation, as in the opinion of Galloway, Howe was unwise not to have attacked the ragged Americans in their winter quarters at Valley Forge. Furthermore, the wisdom underlying Howe's sea invasion of Pennsylvania in 1777 can be seriously questioned. Even Washington would have agreed with many of Galloway's objections. "With a little enterprise and industry," the American commander wrote after the war, the British, on more than one occasion, could have crushed the rebellion.[50]

Galloway's attempts to prop up the sagging British morale for a continuation of the war were hardly isolated efforts. An avalanche of pamphlets followed the collapse of Britain's peace initiative in 1778. A frequent recommendation in many of these essays was that Parliament conduct an investigation of the management of the war. At least four factions desired an inquiry. The opposition elements in the House of Commons hoped an investigation would prove the ministry culpable and lead to the formation of a new government. Some military officers, particularly the Howe brothers and Burgoyne, believed an investigation would clear their names and demonstrate that ministerial decisions were responsible for the military failures. Lord George Germain, the secretary in charge of military planning for the American war, hoped an inquiry would vindicate his policies and fix the responsibility for the American failures on the field officers. Finally, Galloway and other loyalists believed the old military commanders would be removed when their incompetence was demonstrated by the inquiry. Galloway hoped a more efficient corps of officers would emerge and infuse new morale into the nation. On the other hand, the ministry—exclusive of Germain—wished to avoid an inquest. Lord North and the King feared the investigation might lead to political inquiries which could topple the government. Nevertheless, in March 1779 the House of Commons agreed to a motion of Charles James Fox that it form a committee of the whole to investigate the conduct of the war. The subsequent investigation, which lasted from 29 March until late June, was commonly called the Howe Inquiry.[51]

During the inquiry the military officers argued that the resources provided their armies had been inadequate, while Admiral Lord Howe complained that the British fleet was so badly provisioned that parity with the French forces was seldom realized. The commanders also insisted that they were criticized on the one hand as gamblers and reproved on the other hand for being indecisive. General Howe attributed his failures to a multitude of obstacles: he had never been provided with sufficient manpower; the climate had been too hot, or too cold, or too rainy to allow decisive action; the countryside was too barren to accommodate an invading army; the terrain was too often impassable. He suggested that on occasion he had refused to attack the rebels—for example, during Washington's encampment at Valley Forge—because the enemy "did not occasion any difficulties so pressing as to justify an attack." He insisted that it was pointless to attack the colonists unless a certain advantage would result. He thought it senseless to attack merely for the sake of fighting.[52]

General Howe was bitter because he had been attacked for leaving the Hessians to defend Trenton. The mercenaries were experienced soldiers, he argued; furthermore, to transfer them at that time would have disgraced them and broken their morale. Some critics attacked Howe for occupying Philadelphia in 1777 instead of invading New England, but he argued that an invasion of the North would not have been fruitful. A year would have been consumed in occupying the coastal areas alone; in addition, the New England militia was "the most persevering" of all the colonial forces. Moreover, Howe contended that the only way to end the rebellion was to destroy the American army, and by attacking Pennsylvania Howe was assured that Washington would be lured into battle, for the rebel commander would be compelled to defend Congress. Moreover, he insisted, he had been led to believe that he could expect considerable loyalist support in the Delaware Valley, whereas New England was notorious for its minimal number of Tories.[53]

Two aspects of Howe's conduct occasioned great criticism, including attacks in several pamphlets written by Galloway. Howe's roundabout manner of transferring his troops from New York to Philadelphia in 1777 was bitterly assailed. In addition, Howe was attacked for failing to coordinate his movements with Burgoyne, who at the same time was marching into New York from Canada. Howe asserted that the means he used to reach Pennsylvania were dictated by the inadequate strength of his troops. When the operation was planned, he said, he had requested an additional 15,000 troops; this would have brought his total strength to 35,000 men. With these numbers, he claimed, he would have proceeded by land. Instead, the ministry promised just 7,800 additional troops, and only 2,900 of these men had arrived by the date scheduled for embarkation. Consequently, he insisted, his plans were altered, and the army was compelled to proceed by sea. From the outset the morale of his men was low. He invaded via the Chesapeake because the Delaware River was heavily fortified and because he hoped to avoid the summer illnesses of the marshy Delaware River region. Utilization of the Chesapeake, moreover, so alarmed the Virginia and Maryland authorities that their troops were not allowed to join Washington's army until after the Battle of Brandywine. As for not assisting Burgoyne, Howe merely implied that his fellow commander should have been able to fend for himself. Howe regarded it as unnecessary to use two armies to seize Albany. He expected Burgoyne—assisted by Colonel Barry St. Leger and his Indian allies—to defeat the rebels, and he sanguinely believed that by the end of 1777 Britain would control Pennsylvania, Delaware, New Jersey, and all of New York. In such an event Britain would have driven a wedge between New England and its southern allies.[54]

The opposition faction in the Commons—joined by its military allies—sought to blame the wartime failures on ministerial inefficiency and incompetence. They also alleged that Galloway and other pamphleteers who had attacked the military officials were in the pay of certain officials. Some members implied that many of these writers were satraps of Germain. Lord North, alarmed at the attacks and insinuations, attempted to close the inquiry before the ministry was truly jeopardized. He noted that no formal charges had been brought against any military commander and that the statements by the Howe brothers had constituted an ample rebuttal to all libelous charges. Nevertheless, at the request of Germain, who hoped to clearly establish his innocence of all American failures, the inquiry was continued.[55]

Germain testified in his own behalf, and he produced two witnesses to affirm his defense. Major General James Robertson, the former deputy governor of New York, testified—although he had not been in America since the early 1760s; Galloway was Germain's other witness. Neither Germain nor Robertson made any attack upon Britain's military leaders. The key to victory, both thought, was the sizable body of American loyalists. Through its trained army and loyalist allies in the colonies, Britain could still suppress the rebellion. After Robertson asserted that two-thirds of the colonists were zealously faithful to the government of Great Britain, Germain moved that new peace proposals were unnecessary. The majority of the colonists abhorred the rebellion and were shouldering arms for Britain, the minister declared. That very day, he said, he had received information from Governor William Tryon of New York that 7,000 American seamen were serving as privateers against the rebels.[56]

Germain and the ministry, which had by now been thoroughly dragged into the inquiry, believed Galloway to be their key witness. Here was an American loyalist who could testify to the overwhelming pro-British sentiment which existed throughout the colonies. In mid-June Galloway testified for five hours before the House of Commons. He intended to make the same accusations against the military which he had been making in his pamphlets and, in addition, to refute Howe's previous testimony. Before taking the stand he indicated to a friend that he hoped to prove that Howe had perjured himself. Galloway, however, was not given much opportunity to testify freely. After a few preliminary remarks—he charged that the Howe brothers and Burgoyne were incompetent, that the loyalists constituted four-fifths of the American population, and that the war could still be won by Britain—opposition politicians led by Edmund Burke seized the floor and questioned Galloway for two hours about his activities before the war. Burke forced Galloway to admit that he had signed the economic boycott agreement at the First Continental Congress. But to several questions he could give no answers. Had he defended the Coercive Acts? Had he supported the policy of maintaining English troops on colonial soil in times of peace? What portions of the First Congress' declarations had he opposed? Galloway begged forgetfulness as an excuse. Burke, in response, exploded that he could not understand "the reason why you, who are of the law, recollect so well the military transactions of Sir William Howe, and forget

THE LOYALIST MIND

so many civil and legal matters that fell within your cognisance while you was [sic] a member of the Congress." Burke questioned the loyalist at length about his pension, implying pointedly that Galloway was bribed by Germain to pamphleteer and testify during the inquiry. The allegation that Galloway was a paid spokesman of the ministry was not uncommon; in fact many ministerial defenders were subjected to similar accusations.[57]

Burke also questioned Galloway's estimate of the number of loyalist sympathizers in America. This was not just a moot point. The ministry had contended from the beginning of the war that America abounded in loyalists and that the rebellion was supported by a small minority of colonists. With proper strategy and effective British generalship, the government maintained, the rebellion would be suppressed shortly. Those who opposed the continuation of the conflict, however, had grown skeptical of the government's appraisal of loyalist strength. Unable to attack the generals, who were their political allies, the opponents of the war concentrated their attack on the Tories. In actuality, they insisted, few colonists had ever supported Great Britain. Colonel Isaac Barre, for instance, charged that Britain had no friends in America and that the ministry had been duped by the inaccurate reports of a few refugees. It was to the loyalists' "misinformation [that] we might chiefly attribute our disasters in America," he added. Burke similarly contended that the loyalists were to blame for Britain's predicament. It "was our friends in America that had done us all the mischief. Every calamity of the war had arisen from our friends." Burke demanded to know why the loyalists had not overthrown Congress if there was so little pro-war sentiment in America. Furthermore, why had so few loyalists come forward to volunteer as soldiers during the several months that Britain occupied Philadelphia? Galloway responded that the loyalists were powerless to stage a counterrevolution because they had been disarmed during 1775. Moreover, Galloway replied, many genuinely pro-British colonists were reluctant to support England until assured that the British really intended to win the war.[58]

Burke characterized Galloway as a "custom-house" officer pensioned by the ministry. Galloway and his type, Burke continued, would always attempt to prove that most Americans were loyalists in order to induce Britain to wage a perpetual war with the majority of the people of America. If the war continued, Burke asked, what should Britain fight for? If Britain fought for an empire in which parliamentary sovereignty was not recognized, the war would have little appeal in England. If Britain fought for an empire in which America unconditionally submitted to the mother country, the loyalists would be unhappy. Others also belittled Galloway's testimony. One member of the House of Commons said Galloway was a man who had "remembered every military manoeuvre that had, as well as those which had not taken place; but who recollected nothing of his own conduct in the American Congress. . . . [A] man of such memory was very improper . . . to be asked questions."[59]

In June 1779, near the end of the inquiry, two peace proposals from the opposition faction turned the debate from an investigation of past failures to a consideration of whether to continue the conflict. On 11 June Sir William Meredith attacked the policy of fighting and simultaneously offered proposals for peace; he also introduced a resolution calling for the formation of a new ministry which would explore fresh avenues to peace. On 22 June David Hartley, who had seconded Meredith's resolution, introduced a more specific motion. Charging that the ministry had merely pretended to offer peace, he proposed a multifaceted policy. He moved for a cease-fire for ten years as a preliminary to negotiations, suspension of all parliamentary acts respecting America during the period of negotiation, a cease-fire between Great Britain and France, and the withdrawal of all British troops from America in return for an American guarantee of safety to the loyalists. In the ensuing debate the opposition faction supported both resolutions and argued that the war had become a stalemate—some alternative policy to a total subjugation of the colonists must be sought. The core of this faction's argument was that outright military victory was impossible since the Americans were nearly unanimous in their opposition to the imperial doctrines Britain had pursued since 1765. Tangential to this thesis, of course, was the feeling that the ministry had drastically overestimated the strength of colonial loyalism. The ministry, in response to the resolutions, contended that the rebellion was supported by a minority of the colonists. The ministry was willing to consider peace if it could be attained with honor, but it insisted on pursuing the conflict until America sued for peace. In late June both resolutions were defeated. The North government survived to continue the war.[60]

The defeat of these resolutions lessened the opposition's interest in the inquiry. Furthermore, as the debate ended, news arrived that Spain was joining France in the conflict against Great Britain. The final event in the inquiry was to have been the recall of Galloway for questioning by General Howe. Ironically, yet typically, Howe was fifteen minutes late in arriving, and North's majority took this opportunity to suspend the investigation.[61]

From Galloway's point of view the inquiry was inconclusive—the military command had not been radically altered. Yet the inquest was not without significance. The government, with its vote of confidence, was free to pursue the war. In addition, the investigation clearly exposed the government's exaggerated reliance on the concept of loyalist strength. As a result, Germain was politically weakened when it was realized that he had rooted British military strategy on such an illusion. Germain survived the investigation, but he was trapped. Unable to dissociate himself from the loyalists—to do so after the inquiry would have been an admission of failure—he was compelled to plan the remaining operations of the war around the concept of loyalist strength. By dramatically revealing the influence of colonial Toryism on British military strategy, the inquiry inevitably made the subject of loyalism a major issue in the subsequent peace settlement.

The inquiry, however, did little to improve Britain's military position. The blockade the government hoped to impose was never adequately enforced. For some time, moreover, the army was barely active. Eighteen months passed after the abandonment of Philadelphia, for instance, before Clinton undertook a major operation. Then he launched the southern strategy with an invasion at Charleston. During the next two years the adversaries alternately skirmished, maneuvered, and slugged head to head through the Carolinas and into Virginia. At last, in the autumn of 1781, Washington trapped a force of more than 6,000 British troops under the Earl of Cornwallis at Yorktown. After enduring a brief siege, Cornwallis forlornly proposed terms of surrender. Washington agreed to all terms solicited by Cornwallis, except for a provision that the loyalists who had joined the British army were to be spared punishment.

After Yorktown the Commons once more debated Britain's war strategy. Loyalism was again at the heart of the issue. The debate was occasioned by a series of motions introduced by David Conway, a member of the opposition. His motion that the war should no longer be pursued was defeated by a single vote. A second motion, which passed, alleged that prolonged war with the colonies would weaken Britain and prevent the restoration of cordial relations with America. Conway's final motion—which was designed to intimidate loyalist advisors or ministers who seemed willing to consider Tory advice—denounced those who advocated the continuance of the war as "enemies" of Great Britain. Lord Germain fought the resolution. Germain persisted in the belief that loyalist sentiment was plentiful in the colonies, and he added that he would "never be the minister who should give up that dependence" of America on Britain. When he declared that he wished "to leave the [loyalists] their country," a voice from the opposition benches rejoined, "you will leave us no country." Since recent defeats in by-elections had depleted North's majority, the Commons listened more favorably to denunciations of the Tories than to Germain's repetitious apologies. The prevailing view was probably that of John Eardley Wilmot of the opposition. He maintained that the real culprits were "those who have listened to [the Tories] too long, and were convinced by them on a subject, of which they were incompetent judges, because they were parties, and saw it only in partial light." In early March 1782 Conway's third motion passed without a division. The fate of the war, of the North government, and of Galloway and the loyalists was sealed.[62]

The passage of the Conway resolutions and the subsequent collapse of the North ministry silenced Galloway and the loyalists. The colonial exiles offered no further military advice. The controversy over the Tories abated thereafter until the Treaty of Paris was submitted to Parliament in 1783. According to Article Five the United States Congress was to recommend that each state compensate its loyalists for property losses. Many in the House of Lords were critical of this portion of the treaty, arguing that the states could not be depended upon to compensate the loyalists. Some lords who believed Britain should have insisted on a territorial grant from America to the loyalists denounced the treaty as a national disgrace. Most members, however, agreed with the prime minister, Lord Shelburne, that a "part must be wounded, that the whole of the empire may not perish." Shelburne lamented that he had faced a Hobson's choice of accepting those terms or continuing the war. The House of Lords, however, did resolve that Anglo-American friendship hinged on the United States' fulfillment of Article Five.[63]

The House of Commons held a similar debate on the controversial article. Many in the government refused to defend the treaty, although Lord North, now a member of the opposition, led those who opposed it. He intimated that Britain was humiliated by the treaty. The honor of Great Britain, he continued, had been abused by the treatment of the loyalists. He maintained that Britain should have continued to occupy New York, Charleston, and Rhode Island until Congress and the states complied with the treaty. Burke, who had previously been so critical of loyalist tactics, described the treaty as a "gross libel on the national character," and he suggested that Article Five made a mockery of the Treaty's preamble which spoke of reciprocity. Most administration supporters, however, defended the treaty. They argued that Britain could still compensate the loyalists living in exile in England and that the treaty forbade further confiscation of loyalist properties by the Americans. The Commons, however, rejected a resolution strikingly similar to the one adopted by the House of Lords and voted to censure the treaty.[64]

Galloway remained silent during the debates, but once the treaty went into effect he urged Britain to remunerate the loyalists. He realized that American compensation was unlikely. Legally the United States was not required to pay the loyalists; the government of the new nation was merely required to recommend that the states reimburse their victims. Since Britain had recognized the independence of the United States, and since no property had been seized by the rebels until after American independence had been declared, he reasoned that the seizure of loyalist properties

THE LOYALIST MIND

amounted only to confiscation of the possessions of traitors. The loyalists, he insisted, could not hope to be reimbursed by the Americans. Only two hopes existed for restitution. The loyalists could attempt to regain their estates through an appeal to "their unrelenting and triumphant enemies," or they could look to Britain for assistance. Galloway urged Parliament to determine the losses of each loyalist. One could only hope, he added, that Parliament would be kinder to its friends than America was certain to be to its enemies.[65]

The final political pamphlet published by Galloway also dealt with the problem of loyalist claims. In 1787 he once again implored Parliament to assist those who had remained loyal to Britain. He reminded Parliament that by the terms of the social contract the government promised citizens protection in return for allegiance. The loyalists, he said, had never wavered in their allegiance to the crown. Galloway quoted extensively from royal proclamations and parliamentary resolutions to demonstrate that loyalists had been promised protection since the Stamp Act controversy. Britain, he declared, owed the loyalists ·"a debt of the highest and most inviolable nature, from which Parliament can never honourably and justly discharge itself, but by making adequate compensation." Britain could be absolved from its moral obligation to the loyalists only by national insolvency.[66]

The loyalist claims issue was not speedily settled. The government created a commission of inquiry which spent several years investigating the problem. Finally, in 1790 the commission recommended payment of over £3,000,000 to 2,291 loyalist claimants. Galloway was awarded an annual pension of £500. Although "Mr. Galloway was a member of the First Congress," the commission reported, "he endeavored to promote the constitutional dependence of the colonies on Great Britain" and later he "conducted himself as a zealous loyalist and rendered services to the British government."[67]

Galloway was in exile for the remainder of his life. He was never very happy in England. Without his former wealth and status, always regarded as an outsider, he longed to return to America. He found it humiliating, as his daughter noted, to be reduced from a state of affluence to a state where he could "*rejoice* at the bounty of the public." In 1785 he sought the post of chief justice of Nova Scotia, but instead the office was awarded to a member of the loyalist claims commission. Five years later he requested that the Pennsylvania authorities drop all war charges still pending against him. In 1793 he wrote Thomas McKean, the chief justice of Pennsylvania, to beg for readmission to the state. He claimed that he had been driven to loyalism. He had hoped to remain neutral in the Anglo-American conflict following his retirement from public life in 1775, but revolutionary terrorists hounded him until, fearing for his life, he fled to the safety of the British army. Pennsylvania denied his request for clemency.[68]

So Galloway stayed in Britain. He beamed over a satisfactory marriage which he arranged between his daughter and a London aristocrat. But it was a rare triumph. He was lonely in his later years, absorbed in melancholy and almost certainly aware of the repeated jibes American newspapers poked at him. A generation after Yorktown, for instance, an American essayist typically suggested that a fitting statue for all foes of liberty would consist of a god upon whose "right hand they may place [Benedict] Arnold, on his left Galloway." Intellectually, Galloway turned from political to religious diatribes in his declining years; his final pamphlet speculated on biblical prophecies. In 1803 the seventy-three-year-old Galloway died in obscurity in Watford, England.[69]

II

The Loyalist Mind

"One Supreme Politic Mind"

3

Man and Government:

"To promote the public good and safety"

A few years ago in a Pulitzer Prize-winning study, Bernard Bailyn restored
ideas to center stage as a causal factor in the flow of historical events.[1] For
most of this century historians treated ideas cavalierly or superficially. Human behavior, scholars contended, normally resulted from socioeconomic or
political considerations. It is not difficult to see why ideas were not appreciated. Historians writing during the Progressive era or in the midst of the
cataclysmic events of the 1930s naturally assumed that men were more
likely to be motivated by economic desires than by intellectual concerns.
Ideas, it frequently seemed, were to be used solely as tools, as weapons.
Moreover, many were influenced by psychologists who believed that the
real man was to be found in the subconscious, in the inner being; what man
thought, therefore, was either suspect or irrelevant.

But recent studies by social scientists and historians have indicated
that ideas do in fact play a substantive role in the conduct of men. Humans
respond to stimuli according to the manner in which reality is perceived.
Ideas shape and condition responses; ideas, in Gordon Wood's phrase, can
therefore become "historical events in their own right."[2]

In the last few years several studies have demonstrated the influence
of ideas upon the events of the American Revolution. Succinctly stated,
these studies—principally those of Bailyn, Wood, and Maier—argued that
the radicalism of the 1760s and 1770s was the outgrowth of what they
termed "Real Whig" ideology. This school of thought, popularized by English radicals following the Glorious Revolution, stressed the tensions exis-
tent in every society between power and "its natural prey, its necessary
victim," liberty. This ideology held that power in itself was not evil but was

turned into a malevolent force by man's natural "susceptibility to corruption" and his "lust for self-aggrandizement." Liberty, "always weak, always defensive," was therefore in constant peril. Nevertheless, the British, with their "liberty-loving temper," had devised an extraordinary "constitution" capable of successfully controlling power. The success of this constitution "lay in its peculiar capacity to balance and check the basic forces within society." Hence the three social orders within British society were counterpoised against one another. Royalty, nobility, and the commons entered into a "balanced sharing of power." So long as each branch of society fulfilled its assigned role, the other branches would be restrained, and aggression against liberty would be forestalled.[3]

As the century progressed, according to these historians, English radicals increasingly warned that the system of balances was threatened by an alarming deterioration in the British moral fiber—a tragic turn of events which showed itself politically in repeated executive encroachments on the powers of the British legislature. These warnings were taken seriously in the colonies. This "Real Whig" ideology was reenforced by imperial decisions made after 1763. It was, in fact, the "meaning imparted to . . . events after 1763 by this integrated group of attitudes and ideas" which provoked the American Revolution. The colonists suddenly began to see "with increasing clarity, not merely mistaken, or even evil, policies violating the principles upon which freedom rested, but what appeared to be evidence of nothing less than a deliberate assault launched surreptitiously by plotters against liberty both in England and in America." Through such logic, for instance, the colonists observed similarities between the St. George's Field Massacre, an incident in which British troops killed numerous members of a British mob in 1769, and the Boston Massacre, in which British regulars fired on an American crowd in 1770. The heavy-handed manner with which the crown treated John Wilkes, moreover, seemed to parallel its austere policy toward the colonial legislatures. By 1768 the colonists pictured themselves as the proponents of a new libertarian order for mankind and grandiosely considered America to be the final bastion in the war against tyranny. Americans had become "world revolutionaries."[4]

What connection, one might wonder, could exist between the "Real Whig" ideology and Joseph Galloway, between a philosophy which, as Bailyn lucidly demonstrated, produced rebels and a Pennsylvanian who remained a loyalist? The historian is confronted by the inescapable fact that not all colonists were revolutionaries, nor were all activists loyalists. Were the radicals singularly influenced by their intellectual environment, while Galloway and his allies remained unmoved by ideological considerations? If intellectual currents are to be treated as a motivational factor in a historical event, how can one explain such obviously different behavior among the participants?

Is it conceivable that the intellectual atmosphere whose progeny included rebels might also have spawned those willing to risk their lives and property in defense of the empire? Unless we are willing to deny the role of ideas as causal events in history, the possibility of such an occurrence must be conceded. But how can such a development be explained? For one thing, of course, intellectual forces other than those emphasized by Bailyn swirled about the colonies and claimed their adherents. Galloway, for instance, was influenced by "Real Whig" polemics. His writings contain such frequent acknowledgments of Whig imagery that these passages might be mistakenly attributed to a revolutionary zealot. But, much like the radicals, Galloway accepted some Whig concepts and rejected others; he followed some ideals to their logical conclusion, while he merely trifled with other notions.

Galloway's ideas were, like those of most men, a diverse composite of the intellectual trends of his era. He came of age in bustling, invigorating Philadelphia, a provincial capital caught in the intellectual crosscurrents of the empire. European ideas drifted into this cosmopolitan enclave, sometimes to mingle with the rustic notions of the New World, sometimes to conflict with the realities of the primitive colonial environment. From the study in his fashionable Market Street home, from his legal chambers, and from his lofty seat in the Assembly, Galloway observed the tempo of the age. His pamphlets and essays reveal the impact of John Locke, but also the influence of Samuel Pufendorf, Hugo Grotius, and Thomas Hobbes. The works of the English legalists, particularly Sir William Blackstone, colored his thought. He read Niccoló Machiavelli, but Jean Jacques Burlamaqui was more influential.

Ideas do not exist in a vacuum. Since they are a means of explaining one's existence, it is logical that both the exponent of an idea and the idea itself are conditioned by one's environment. In short, men embrace those concepts which are meaningful to them. Most enlightened men in the eighteenth century, for instance, argued that either an excessively powerful ruler or an excessively libertarian society tended to endanger sound government. Some, however, were more alarmed at the former prospect, others at the latter. Frequently an idea suggests one notion to one person, but a decidedly different notion to another. For example, most colonists believed that liberty was synonymous with balanced government. Some persisted in thinking that balanced government of necessity must resemble the English model; others grew to believe that alternative means of balancing a government existed.

Like his adversaries, Galloway acted largely in the light of his experiences and the manner in which he perceived events after 1765. After the Stamp Act controversy his principles, instead of modifying with events, seemed to harden and grow less flexible. His ideology, which he consistently manifested, dictated his responses to street mobs and the agitation of popular colonial leaders, structured his reaction to imperial legislation and colonial dissent. His philosophy followed a logical growth pattern. His attitudes toward human behavior colored his ideas about the proper mode of government. His concept of good government influenced his stance toward Britain and the colonies and assisted in the formation of a philosophy as to the best means of governing the empire. This chapter will analyze the first step in his pattern of logic—his philosophy of man and government.

If it is understood that Galloway's thought crystallized during the early phases of the Anglo-American impasse and remained static thereafter, the complexities of his mind can be seen and his behavior better comprehended. Galloway then can be perceived in a new light. His assertion of loyalty to Great Britain no longer seems merely the act of an opportunist; his conduct no longer seems characterized by equivocation. His actions throughout the upheaval were logical and rational. The choices he ultimately made were almost predictable.

To understand the mind of Galloway, one must begin with his attitude toward man and man's attempt to govern himself. Everything else in Galloway's intellectual makeup flowed from the conclusions he reached in this realm.

Man, he argued, was by nature a selfish creature. All his mannerisms and vices sprang from his instinct of self-interest. But it was an idiosyncrasy of man to be burdened by dual and paradoxical elements within his nature. On the one hand, he loved personal gain. This universal drive in man generated competition, which in turn provoked malice between self-indulgent, egoistic species and made struggle inevitable. Man had a tendency to engage in questionable acts to satiate his limitless ambitions. "That which we love and engages our attention," Galloway maintained, "we are ever ready to purchase at any *price*." Man was so enslaved by greed that he could not "enjoy freedom of judgment, scarcely freedom of thought." It was an uncommon man who was so incorruptible as to successfully resist the "enticing baits of honor and interest. . . . [He is] among mankind as a comet among the stars, rarely to be seen."[5]

But man's perversity brought forth a conflicting desire, a self-preserving hope for personal security. Although man was a greedy and aggressive creature, he also needed protection from like creatures. Reconciling this opposition in the nature of man became the central task of the political theoretician, for a drive which compelled man to both acquisitiveness and security tended to produce an "intolerable avarice and a base dereliction of duty." The species was all too willing to surrender its freedom, to remain servile to any ruler who promised that which was the object of its lust.[6]

Like most English and colonial contemporaries, Galloway believed man had created government to control his selfish instincts and to obstruct his otherwise inevitable slide into a cannibalistic social environment. Man, he thought, had consciously and ceremoniously invented society to escape the chaos and treachery of primitive nature. The study of antiquity, he asserted, revealed that the original design of government was the protection of people and property from oppression. Since in nature the weak became the prey of the strong, man created civil society for the common defense. It soon became obvious, however, that man required protection from foreign as well as domestic violence. Man did not form only one society, Galloway believed, but because of environmental circumstances was driven to form different societies. Hence, on an international plane the weaker again were victimized by the ambition and aggression of the more powerful.[7]

Galloway accepted without reservation most eighteenth-century theories regarding the social contract. When governments were established, he acknowledged, rulers and ruled entered into a reciprocal agreement. The social contract implied not only a delegation of power to the rulers—for the purpose of promoting the public well-being—but an assumption of magisterial restraint. Governmental powers therefore were limited, and all acts of government which burst the bonds of the contract were "*void in themselves.*" For their part of the bargain, subjects agreed to surrender the fundamental liberties they had enjoyed in nature and promised to swear allegiance to the polity. On one substantive matter Galloway took issue with the commonplace Whig understanding of the social contract. He did not consider the natural rights of man to be inviolate. Whereas most Whigs believed that man's innate rights endured following the institution of society, Galloway argued that man surrendered his natural rights upon the conclusion of the social contract. Following this momentous surrender of intrinsic liberties, man derived all rights from the state; these prerogatives were the reward of submission and obedience. The abrogation of these rights constituted a restraint on the liberties of individuals for the welfare of the whole. Galloway believed governments endured so long as both parties adhered to the two covenants in the original contract. He was untroubled by the implications of disloyalty by subjects, but severance of the original contract by the ruled was a thornier issue, and Galloway, like most contemporary theoreticians, was careful not to become too entangled in the intricacies of that problem. Only when the government had acted arbitrarily and when it had been repeatedly petitioned without success to alter its ways, he thought, could the citizens consider the contract nullified. "There is no truth more evident," he concluded, "than that . . . if either party refuse the performance on his part, the other is discharged."[8]

Galloway realized that the surrender of individual natural rights in order to establish government was not without risk. Government improperly conceived could be as dangerous as the state of nature from which social beings hoped to escape. He believed that government must rest, in the final analysis, on either "fear or art." To be truly effective a ruler must command "fear and respect." But if a despotic power based on fear and motivated by pecuniary interest gained ascendancy, the result would inevitably be constant turmoil. Liberty would gradually disintegrate until, "fatigued with Controversy and Oppression," the ruled agreed to "servilely submit to the will and Pleasure" of the rulers. Subject to the mercy of a despot, the property of the governed would be as insecure as before the creation of the state. In its own way a weak and ineffectual government, an organic structure incapable of providing the protection sought by the governed, was every bit as dangerous as a despotic polity. Galloway maintained that power entrusted to "feeble hands" resulted unavoidably in acts of "injustice, ambition, and oppression." The result was disrespect "which would soon ripen into contempt; the consequences whereof . . . is, we have the name of a government, but no safety or protection under it." Soon people and property were rendered defenseless. The problems of irresolute governments were heightened by modern, pluralistic societies. Factionalism produced a perpetual competition for power, and this struggle could destroy the unity and harmony of society. Unless government was sufficiently resilient to control these diverse groups, chaos was inevitable.[9]

Knowing these risks, Galloway devoted considerable attention to the ancient puzzle of jurisdiction. He felt that men must be aware of certain natural laws, or "general laws," in order to structure sound governments. All government must, for instance, have what he variously referred to as "a *supreme Authority*—a supreme Power of Decision," a "supreme will," or—the phrase he borrowed from Locke—a "legislative power." It was this will or authority, this essence of sovereignty, which enabled the state "to bind, cement, and tie together *every Part* or *Member*." Societies simply could not exist devoid of sovereignty. By nature all societies consisted of a "Head" as well as others of "greater and less Utility, Dignity and Importance." Unity, therefore, was possible only when a society acknowledged the imperative virtues of supremacy and subordination.[10] It

is this only which can give to society a consistency of Laws, Regulation and Policy; which diffuses a similarity of Customs Habits and Manners, which fixes the national attachment and establishes an uniformity of Principle and Conduct. . . . And it is this Unity in the supreme power of Government which only can enable it to Collect and Command the whole strength of the several parts of the Society for its preservation and defense.[11]

It was imperative, moreover, that the inhabitants of the subordinate dominions share the "same fundamental rights and privileges" as those enjoyed in the sovereign entity. Furthermore, citizens of lesser units must be guaranteed the right to "partake of the supreme power of the state." Inequities fostered mistrust and apprehension which, in turn, jeopardized the sovereign polity. "Every distinction," he asserted, "must be offensive and odious, and cannot fail to create uneasiness and jealousies, which will ever weaken the government, and frequently terminate in insurrections." The problem was particularly acute in societies where the citizens resided "in regions . . . very remote from each other." If distinctions were permitted in such polities, separatist movements would inevitably emerge, and the cherished "union and harmony" of the state could not be expected to "long subsist." If the sovereign power was at the apex of society, it was reasonable to assume that the remainder of the structure was composed of subordinate bodies. Every member of society, "whether political, official, or individual, must be subordinate to [the] supreme will." Only the sovereign power could create an inferior polity, an entity which was "restrained and limited in a variety of instances, by the express words of the grant under the authority of which it has been established." Ordinarily, such a political subdivision was "supreme within its own circle" only, and its general authority was limited to regulating its own police powers.[12]

For Galloway, as for most of his contemporaries, another rule of proper government was that political power should be utilized only by those who possessed property. This was an "antient Maxim," as true for the Romans and Anglo-Saxons as for his own generation. Power, he asserted, "naturally results from Property and Estates" because they are "the most permanent and unchangeable . . . and therefore the most worthy of protection." The "supreme will" of which Galloway spoke, therefore, was the consensus of the propertied interests in the state.[13]

An additional phenomenon which Galloway emphasized was the certain clash between liberty and authority. The constitutional arrangements agreed upon by rulers and ruled were constantly jeopardized by man's natural imperfections. The ruled, he feared, would always strive for greater freedom than permitted by the original charter; the rulers would inevitably conspire for increased powers. The clash posed a deadly threat to the foundations of society. Freedom was power—the power of the individual to act as he pleased. Unwarranted freedom, like unlicensed power for officeholders, would result in tyranny. In the one fatal perversion, the masses' incessant groping for additional liberties would erode the proper authority of the ruled until disorder and chaos prevailed. In the other, excessive power placed in the hands of even the most charitable of men brought the risk of governmental oppression. An improper check of power and liberty, he suggested, bore "an Analogy to a Ship without Rudder, Rigging, or Sails." Whichever perversion triumphed, "the Condition of mankind would be little mended" by the social contract, for men would "scarcely [be] better than in the original State of Nature and Confusion, before any civil Polity was agreed on."[14]

Still another maxim of proper government was that "certain laws and establishments" existed which were "peculiar to each particular form, on which its constitution and essence depend." He thought four styles of government were possible: monarchy, aristocracy, democracy, and mixed government. Each style required elements "which were as inconsistent with those of a different form, as the rulers peculiarly necessary in building a house are with those in building a ship." As with "all works of nature," each form of government required a "systematical combination . . . of principles and parts, which determines its species." Should nature's way be short-circuited, utter confusion was the inevitable result. Absolute monarchies therefore required the rule of only one man; aristocracies, the rule of only one privileged order. Democracies implied the participation of all citizens. A mixed or balanced government allotted one branch of the polity to each type of social order. Care must be taken, moreover, to ensure that subordinate governments were not based on dissimilar principles, lest these governments corrupt the sovereign government.[15]

These maxims, Galloway insisted, offered convincing evidence that men could, through rational inquiry, construct a viable state secure from the natural enemies of sound rule. Nevertheless, hazards were always present. Threats to stable, orderly government were inherent in every possible polity and lurked within every stratum of society. For instance, each form of government contained inherent defects. The most deadly threat to stability, he believed, was posed by democracy—the government championed by the restless, ambitious masses. And, according to Galloway, the peculiarities of American society increased the threat posed by this element. The ambitions of the lower economic classes were not only heightened by conditions in the colonies, but these classes had actually gained an influence in political affairs which was not allowed their European and British counterparts. The unsettled nature of America, with its great, free landmass, ensured the existence of an enormous, propertied—and hence enfranchised—lower-class element. These same features had gradually leavened colonial society, so that the traditional lines of social authority were imperiled. The colonists thus were poised on the horns of a dilemma. More than any other people, Americans were faced with the fatal choice between democracy and autocracy.[16]

Galloway refused to consort with the growing number of colonists who extolled the virtues of the lower orders and who argued that government grounded on rule by the people would usher in a new era of political stability. He remained unmoved and continued to loathe and fear the common man. He usually described commoners as "ignorant and violent," as the "unthinking, ignorant multitude." Most of his political concepts stemmed from a desire to check their "lawless ambition" and to keep their "licentiousness in awe."[17]

Although Galloway believed that the differences between the social classes inevitably bred misunderstanding, his varied diagnoses of the factors which produced political ferment were muddled and inconsistent. At times he seemed to argue that the social classes were locked in a deadly struggle growing out of economic greed. Because of their alleged stolid and doltish nature, he feared at times that the masses would always be susceptible to the demagogue and ever ready to scale the "ladder of ambition." Yet, he more often thought of the masses as normally tranquil and as creatures of "habit and fixt manners" who easily accommodated themselves to any form of government under which they lived. Even those who had the misfortune to be reared in arbitrary and despotic polities were "not easily drawn into a dereliction" against their government. "A fish spawned and bred in muddy water," he advised, "abhors the crystal stream." Nevertheless, greedy agitators drawn from the "better sort" would always be capable of seducing a few of the "disloyal menaces" among the people. Historically, trouble flared when "a few artful, bold and ambitious men" succeeded in their efforts "to delude the licentious and restless few, which every society affords, into arms."[18]

Alarming events in his own time—the Paxton incident or the nearly unceasing turmoil which had upended Pennsylvania politics since 1765— only strengthened his belief that society continually tottered on the precipice. He was continuously haunted by images of

> companies of armed, but undisciplined men, headed by men unprincipled, travelling over your estates, entering your houses—your castles—and sacred repositories of safety for all you hold dear and valuable—seizing your property, and carrying havoc and devastation wherever they head—ravishing your wives and daughters, and afterwards plunging the dagger into their tender bosoms, while you are obliged to stand the speechless, the helpless spectators.[19]

Democratic government therefore was the least attractive form of governance in the estimation of Galloway. He did not distinguish between republican and democratic polities. Each was commonly characterized by scenes of "disorder and confusion"; each was "perpetually liable to all the mischiefs of faction, discord and confusion." Such governments were weak and incapable of preserving either the internal or external peace of their subjects. Discord in a democracy resulted from frequent changes of rulers;

the normally placid masses, he thought, were made tumultuous by a "factious, weak, and confused" government. But the suppression of the democratic inclinations of the masses held little appeal for Galloway. Such a policy resulted in "the arrogance of power" and led the oppressed to "resent the illiberal and odious distinctions made between them and the other members of the State."[20]

Nor did the establishment of an unchecked monarchy or an unhindered aristocracy enthrall Galloway. The transition from monarchy to tyranny, he feared, was "easy, natural, and certain." Rule by a privileged aristocratic order, on the other hand, inevitably resulted in despotism or chaos. Tyranny resulted when the ruling class remained united; whenever the elite class divided and competed for power, the state was weakened and anarchy resulted. Yet authoritarian rule could not be imposed without some popular support. "Arbitrary power," he admonished, "will ever have Numbers to support it; without, Power could not become arbitrary."[21]

A remedy for these potential malfunctions of government existed, however, and the constitution of the parent state—an unwritten constitution—pointed the way. Like the "skilful physician" who blended various potions in order to cure dangerous illnesses, British statesmen in the preceding century had fused the essentials of each type of government so as to obtain "natural liberty perfectly and justly regulated." Galloway thought the English government was unique. It was a "mixed form," composed partly of the principles of monarchy, aristocracy, and democracy. Two aspects of balanced governments, he concluded, softened the evils of other forms of government. First, an excess of power by one branch would be checked by the other branches. The aristocratic and democratic branches, for instance, could hinder the tyrannous inclinations of the monarchy; or the monarchy and aristocracy might stop the natural tendency of democracy to degenerate into chaos. Second, a government of equilibrium was sturdy because of its inclusion of the people—by which Galloway meant the propertied interests—in the governing process. If the people "compose a part of the supreme authority," he exclaimed, "its foundation will be solid, and its continuance permanent . . . because the people themselves, who are interested in its preservation, partake of the power which is necessary to defend it."[22]

Like most Whig ideologists, he believed each branch of the British government represented a separate social order. The King personified monarchy; the House of Lords was the organ of the aristocracy; the House of Commons was the voice of the people. But the American's concept of the structure of mixed government was not entirely consistent with that of all other contemporary theorists. Some Whigs, in the aftermath of the Revolution of 1688, regarded the monarchy as an essentially executive institu-

THE LOYALIST MIND

tion. Others, including Galloway, believed the monarch fulfilled a dual role. Since the reign of Henry VIII the monarch, together with the two houses of Parliament, had constituted the "supreme legislative head" of the state. The monarch therefore shared in the law-making processes. It was, in fact, this ingenious attempt to unite the will of all branches so they " 'should never desire *but one and the same thing*, in whatever relates to the end and purpose of society' " which distinguished the British state and controlled the otherwise natural inclination toward factionalism and upheaval. Hence the nation was " 'animated by *one soul*' " and achieved a uniform national behavior.[23]

In addition to the "King . . . legislative," the monarch was also an executive officer. In this capacity the sovereign acted as "an indifferent, disinterested, and independent power." He was, moreover, the representative and trustee of the legislature, the agent designated with the task of superintending the preservation of the society, and the official responsible for restoring, "whenever enervated, the true principles of the constitution to their perfect balance and former energy."[24]

The monarch therefore occupied a crucial and even dangerous position in a balanced polity. He was the watchdog of the system, and his double role seemingly afforded him a perfect opportunity to subvert the general will. However, Galloway believed he understood how best to constrain the monarchy. Under the British constitution the " '*King can do no wrong*,' " he counseled. Such a maxim meant only that in the political realm the monarch could vitiate neither the constitution nor the trust placed in him, and should he err, the mistake would be imputed to his counselors. Moreover, any kingly act inconsistent with the law was "void in itself." He thought this a perfect remedy against anarchy or tyranny, for the dignity of the office would be preserved at the same time the officeholder was effectively contained within safe bounds.[25]

Galloway maintained that the constitution specifically prevented the monarch from engaging in certain activities. The sovereign executive, for instance, could not unilaterally alter the constitution. Nor could he reduce the powers of any organ in the state. He could neither create courts which might interfere with the jurisdiction of established courts nor conceive new agencies and posts inconsistent with the laws of the nation. He was forbidden to appoint officials for life terms, lest such an official "deprive the sovereign executive power . . . of its superintendence, check and controul, over the illegal and licentious conduct of the servants of the Crown." Finally, the monarch was forbidden to establish inferior communities with powers independent of the state or to permit inferior bodies to act in an insubordinate manner.[26]

Some contemporaries—most notably Baron Charles Montesquieu—

believed a direct correlation existed between geography and good government. National geography, many alleged, conditioned people for governments of a certain nature; all governments, some thought, functioned more satisfactorily in a small region. But Galloway scoffed at these notions and maintained that as the body's extremities obeyed the heart and brain, quality government functioned without heed to the magnitude of the state. "It is the Uniformity and Vigor in Government which constitutes and transmits its power equally through all the parts of Society." And, of course, in the estimation of Galloway a well-run balanced government possessed the greatest uniformity and vigor in its operations.[27]

Although the balanced state afforded the most safety from disturbance, it, too, was precariously perched on the thin line which separated stability from chaos. Struggle between the component elements of the body politic was inevitable. Should the contest become acute, or should the balance fail to control the warring factions, "the state must suffer severe convulsions" and probably even "total ruin." Then, the peril of rule by a tyrant was enhanced. The monarch, through demagoguery or control of the military and judicial functions of the state, might simply overwhelm the other branches and assert his will. The greater likelihood, however, was the establishment of despotism through the back door. Galloway thought the most grave threat to mixed government was constituted by the democratic branch. Should

> the *many* assume to themselves the direction of affairs, claiming [it] from an inherent and natural right,—tyranny will be the consequence.—The tyranny of the people is the most violent and bloody, though of the shortest duration, for the evils it introduces are so severely felt, that they soon grow weary of it themselves, and throw the whole power into the hands of some popular man, to skreen them from themselves, and he repays them in their own coin, as soon as he feels the power which, without restriction or limitation, they rashly and injudiciously confer upon him. [Hence,] tumult is a certain introduction to arbitrary power.[28]

Although institutional strength would help preserve good government, the people themselves ultimately had to resist tyranny. Galloway was confident that most men could be persuaded that balanced government was in their best interest. It "is education alone which forms and fixes human habits, manners, attachments, and aversions. . . . So men, educated in the principles of one form of government, will ever esteem and prefer it." Fear, however, was essential as well. The law must be uniform throughout the polity, he asserted, and the law must be enforced. In this manner laws would be "lessons of instruction, by which every subject is daily taught his duty and mode of obedience to the State."[29]

Within the parameters of eighteenth-century colonial thought, Galloway's concept of good government was not uncommon. His viewpoint stemmed from a belief that man's characteristic greed must be controlled and subordinated to the welfare of the entire human species. Men were torn, he thought, between an acquisitive instinct and the instinct for personal security. Society and government were created by men to reconcile these divergent forces. Government, therefore, was the product of a dual contract between men seeking social order and a covenant between the rulers and the ruled. The ultimate bargain in the social contract was that man would surrender his natural rights and offer compliance to the state in return for the protection afforded by the state. But the system was workable, Galloway stressed, only if the polity was "limited and restrained" in the sway it exercised over the ruled. The problem, therefore, was to establish a polity sufficiently powerful to provide protection but sufficiently "restrained" to prevent the emergence of tyrannical governors. The answer to this puzzle, he thought, was to establish a balanced state, a system in which the three classic forms of government—monarchy, aristocracy, and democracy—were counterpoised and in which the major factions within society were represented, checked, and balanced. This balanced polity must be sovereign to be effective. In fact, if government lacked sovereignty, society lacked government. Ultimately, however, selfish mankind would have to make the system workable, and Galloway remained confident that man's desire for security would, in the end, triumph over his inveterate greed. But a measure of indoctrination, fear, and law were also required, in his estimation, to control man's imperfect nature.

Galloway's ideology differed in some respects from that expressed by other contemporary writers, but it was hardly a radical deviance. On the surface, moreover, his philosophical theorems provide few clues to his eventual behavior during the Revolution. Whereas most Americans who accepted these dictums turned against Great Britain, Galloway remained loyal. Most radicals discovered cracks in the splendid British system they had once so fervently embraced. Step by step they grew alarmed at the magnitude of the British corruption, at the nefarious designs which they were convinced the ministry harbored against the colonies, at the increasing culpability of the Monarch in the plot to abuse America. Galloway, however, perceived none of this. No hint exists in any of his writings that he ever concluded that Britain was irretrievably—or even uncommonly—corrupt. Despite his symptoms of paranoia, there is no hint that he ever suspected the crown and ministry of a diabolical plot to enslave the colonists.

Unlike his adversaries, Galloway was alarmed by the events in the colonies, not those in the parent state. It was, to paraphrase Bailyn, the meaning which Galloway, as a result of his attitudes and ideas, imparted to events in the colonies after 1765 which drove him to seek solace in the arms of Great Britain. The paroxysm of violence which accompanied the opposition to imperial measures made Galloway more anxious than did the measures themselves. The objectionable legislation might be revoked, but mob activity was difficult to control. Nor was it British degradation so much as American corruption which threatened the fabric of society. The "wisdom and sound policy" of Great Britain had "kept the licentious in awe, and rendered them subservient to their own, and the public welfare." But now the "perfect idea of civil liberty, and free government, such as is enjoyed by the subject in Great-Britain" was jeopardized by the activities of the colonists. The "instruments to trample on the sacred laws of your country" were designed in America, not in Britain. Galloway felt that the American radicals had destroyed private security, the very reason for government. Under the American governments one could never expect protection from "the arbitrary and lawless power of the state."[30]

One cannot come to grips with the essential Galloway until his philosophy is understood. But to scrutinize Galloway's political ideals and his accompanying anxiety at affairs of state in the colonies is to explore only the tip of an iceberg. The Anglo-American conflict hinged on imperial questions, and Galloway's imperialistic ideology, more than any other aspect of his intellectual makeup, affords an explanation for his loyalism.

4

To Preserve the Union:
"There can be but one supreme power"

The central crisis of Galloway's career stemmed from America's nationalistic challenge to British imperial sovereignty. Galloway was hardly impervious to the dynamism of nationalistic concepts—he was, in fact, an Anglo-American nationalist who cherished his peculiar circumstances. He was a citizen of Great Britain; he was at home in the New World; and he dreamed of the glowing economic future which awaited the imperial partners.

Galloway's eventual loyalism has been attributed to his supposed quality as an idle, provincial dreamer; he has also been depicted as a frenzied, desperate politician. Instead, his behavior was the logical culmination of his political ideology. The ultimate factor in Galloway's nationalistic outlook was his perception of empire, a concept which grew logically from his notions concerning the character of man and his government. The principles, he thought, which made for good government on a national scale should also ensure a sound imperial polity. Although he perceived imperfect elements in the superstructure, Galloway thought Britain's imperial government afforded the most secure bulwark against man's insatiable self-indulgence. It was the crystallization of these sentiments in the 1760s which compelled Galloway to regard the radical colonial rhetoric as unpersuasive and dangerous.

During the heat of Anglo-American troubles, Galloway devised a series of plans which he believed could preserve the union and eradicate the worst features of the prerevolutionary imperial polity. He offered a unique solution to the impasse. His schemes envisioned a government similar in many respects to that ultimately designed for the United States in 1787, and the logic he employed to defend his grand design frequently resembled that utilized by the Federalists a decade later.

The central issue which gnawed at the vitals of the empire after 1765 was the extent of British hegemony over the colonies. Did the British government, for instance, possess sovereign legislative powers over the colonists? Traditionally, theorists had insisted that every state required some incontestable final authority. Otherwise, civil strife was inevitable. Thomas Hutchinson, the lieutenant governor of Massachusetts throughout most of the final decade before the rebellion, expressed the British position when he remarked that "no line . . . can be drawn between the supreme authority of Parliament and the total independence of the colonies." At first, the colonists shrank from such a conclusion. The Massachusetts Assembly, for instance, reproved Hutchinson. It insisted that some middle point must exist, for Massachusetts intended to be neither oppressed by nor independent of Britain. For a time some Americans were willing—in the face of British denials that such an expedient was possible—to concede certain powers to Parliament. During the Stamp Act crisis, for example, some believed that Parliament could legitimately levy "external" taxes on the colonies but denied its right to enact "internal" duties for America. Franklin was one of the first to recognize the absurdity of such an argument—in fact, he reached the same conclusion as Hutchinson. Either "Parliament has a right to make *all laws* for us, or . . . it has a power to make *no laws* for us." If the latter expedient were true, he added, "the colonies would then be so many separate states, only subject to the same king, as England."[1]

By the time the Continental Congress met, most colonists agreed that a state could have but one indivisible legislative authority. What remained to be debated, however, was whether Parliament or each colonial assembly constituted that sovereign authority. By 1774 some colonists, including Thomas Jefferson and John Adams, argued that Parliament had no power to legislate for America. The empire hung on the slender thread of the monarchy, since it was with that ruler only that each colony had made its original social contract. Under such an interpretation the assembly of each colony in effect became a parliament. Each colony was virtually an independent state, united with Britain only by a common sovereign king.[2]

In Pennsylvania, John Dickinson best expressed this point of view in a strident response to Galloway's *Candid Examination*. Dickinson agreed that in each "state of society, there must be somewhere a power lodged to make laws obligatory on all members of that society"; this "legislative power," he further agreed, "should be supreme over the members," for otherwise "an end of government" would result. The sovereign legislature in Pennsylvania, Dickinson continued, was the colonial assembly. Its "power, within the bounds of the Province, [was] as supreme, and as unlimited as the power of the Legislature of Great Britain" was within Great Britain. He insisted that each society could have but one legislature; to acknowledge multiple legislative authorities was absurd, an impossibility in a sovereign state. And "of course, the legislature of Great Britain is not the legislature of Pennsylvania," he conjectured. It "would be 'irregular and monstrous' to suppose us subject to two legislatures." Dickinson admitted that the British monarch continued to legitimately exert authority over America, but he denied that the king could wield any legislative powers. The monarch was "vested with the executive power of this Government" only. He was "the representative of our whole state, to see that our laws are duly carried into execution." It was only to this monarchical authority, he insisted, that America continued to demonstrate affection and allegiance.[3]

The First Continental Congress, a prudent political body, did not go quite so far in its public pronouncements. The delegates declared that the English colonists were not represented and could never be properly represented in Parliament. Since Parliament therefore could not legally tax America, the colonists were entitled to exercise unrestricted powers, including the powers of taxation, within their provincial jurisdictions. However, the Congress agreed that Parliament could regulate imperial trade, including the trade of the colonists, in order to promote the common good. Congress further agreed that the colonies were subject to all parliamentary laws passed before the colonization of America was undertaken. Britain's additional imperial powers were vested in the crown and included the power to repeal colonial legislation, appoint colonial executive officials, and hear judicial appeals from the colonists.[4]

Galloway was appalled at the suggestions of America's more radical polemicists and alarmed at the congressional declarations. The insinuation that a "distinction [existed] between a right in parliament to legislate for the colonies, and a right to tax them" was "indefensible," he thought. Parliament was sovereign in all respects. Despite "the most wild and chimerical superstructures" invented by the radicals, the Anglo-American quarrel remained "a dispute between the supreme authority of the state, and a number of its members."[5]

He fell back on the traditional theory of sovereignty: "There is no position more firmly established, in the conduct of mankind, than that there must be in every state a supreme legislative authority, universal in its extent, over every member." Galloway relied on several authorities to demonstrate that in any political entity there could be but one sovereign. He quoted Locke to assert that " 'the first *fundamental positive law* of all commonwealths is . . . [that] there can be but one supreme power.' " He relied on Burlamaqui to show that the " 'state is a body, or society, animated by *one soul*.' " It was foolish to ever consider "inferior communities with rights,

powers, and privileges independent of the State; because this would be . . .
to establish an *imperium in imperio*, a State within a State, the greatest of all
political MONSTERS!"[6]

It was folly, Galloway continued, to pretend to submit to the crown
while denying certain powers of Parliament. The various branches of the
British government combined to constitute "one supreme politic head."
The monarch was not supreme, but merely "one of three equal in power."
The monarch represented the Parliament and "*derives* all his powers" from
that body. To recognize the monarch as the King of Great Britain was
tantamount to a promise of obedience to British laws. However, he queried,
if Congress meant to acknowledge the monarch merely as the King of
America, then "when did he assume that title, and by whom was it
conferred?"[7]

Galloway thought the monarch's claim to govern America as part of
Great Britain was founded on sound logic. Like a nation-state, an empire
was the outgrowth of the social contract. Whereas man formed society to
escape the ravishment of nature, nation-states constructed empires as a
result of their compulsion for security. America, he asserted, had been
discovered and claimed for Britain by explorers acting under the seal of the
King of England. That domain consequently was the property of England.
The colonies carved out of this territory were chartered by the government
of England. Those Englishmen, therefore, who migrated to such a depen-
dency never left society and entered the state of nature, but simply moved
from one part of the realm to another. The social contract was no more
sundered than it would have been when a citizen moved from London to
Bristol. The colonists remained subject to Britain's jurisdiction; they
brought their political rights and obligations to America, including the
requirement of "perfect obedience" to English laws. Galloway was
confident that the alien who moved to a colony, simply by his voluntary
decision to live under the English system, came under the auspices of the
social contract. "They have," he said, citing Locke to prove his point, "by
their own act become subjects; and owe obedience to its laws, as fully as any
other members."[8]

Moreover, the colonial charters reaffirmed the original social contract. To Galloway, colonial charters were similar to the charters of incorporation received by some English cities from the sovereign rulers. These
charters usually conferred some powers on the subordinate government. For
example, London was authorized to enact laws that were necessary for the
well-being of the city—but no one presumed London to be independent of
England. Similarly, although the colonial charters delegated certain powers
to the American governments, all rational men acknowledged that these
were limited powers which could in no manner contravene British author-

ity. Every colonial official, Galloway continued, avowed this state of affairs in the oath of loyalty he swore to the crown. Such a contract, he quoted from Burlamaqui, constituted a ceremonial surrender of the " '*strength* and *will*' " of each member of the society to the " '*will* and *head*' " of the state. These oaths acknowledged the monarch, in the words of Locke, as " '*supreme executor of the law*, made by a joint power of *him* and *others*.' "[9]

The colonists, Galloway alleged, had conceded parliamentary sovereignty by yielding obedience to all the British statutes enacted before the Anglo-American dispute. This, he thought, constituted an admission made by generations spanning 150 years that the colonial assemblies were inferior to the imperial polity. How then, he inquired, could America suddenly refuse to acknowledge the authority of Parliament? Was "something lately discovered, which has convinced them of their mistake," he asked. Only the charters—these original social contracts—could have discharged the colonists from the responsibility to obey parliamentary enactments. But that was hardly the case. He could "discover no exemption . . . in any of them"; in fact, every charter "expressly retain [ed] the submission of the subject to the British laws."[10]

Galloway treated the congressional contention that the colonial assemblies possessed nearly unlimited powers as an absurdity. He did, however, acknowledge that many nation-states had more than one legislature and that the inferior assemblies possessed certain limited police powers. Nevertheless, the sovereign powers of the central government remained unquestioned.[11]

Galloway thus concluded that the dictates of sovereignty required either American subordination to Parliament or an American proclamation of independence. If Parliament was not sovereign in all matters of imperial policy, he told the Continental Congress, the "Law of Great Britain dont bind us in any Case whatsoever."[12] The legislative authority, he concluded

> must of necessity be *equally supreme over all its members*. That to divide this supremacy, by allowing it to exist in some cases, and not in all, over a part of the members, and not the whole, is to weaken and confound the operations of the system and to subvert the very end and purpose for which it was formed; in as much as the vigour and strength of every machine, whether mechanical or political, must depend upon the consistency of its parts, and their corresponding obedience to the supreme *acting power;* And it would have shewn that there can be no alternative; either the colonies must be considered as complete members of the state, or so many distinct communities, in a state of nature, as independent of it, as France or Spain.[13]

To acknowledge the sovereignty of Parliament, however, was not to deny the violation of American rights that had been committed or that the empire could not benefit from repair. The main ingredient of English liberty, he thought, was the right of representation in the sovereign assembly. If the citizenry was unrepresented, the legislators would be unable to enact just or adequate laws. America sent no representatives to Parliament; for that matter, the colonists had no voice in the transaction of imperial business. The colonists therefore were "at the disposal of an absolute power, without the least security." The British government, Galloway asserted, was "as absolute and despotic" toward America "as any Monarch whatever, who singly holds the legislative authority." Colonial subjects must possess the power to consent to all legislative enactments. Since medieval days English citizens who possessed a forty-shilling freehold could vote for legislators. An imperial legislature, consequently, which included no Americans, lacked the power to levy taxes on the colonists.[14]

Galloway admitted that the rights of Americans were violated by more than British taxation policies. The subjects of the empire, he insisted, should enjoy the same fundamental rights and privileges whether they lived in England or America. "Every distinction . . . must be offensive and odious." He objected to commercial and manufacturing prohibitions peculiar to the colonies, although he conceded that some central economic control was necessary for the imperial welfare. He was chagrined that judges were permitted terms of life tenure in Britain, while in the colonies the judiciary served at the pleasure of the crown. He surmised, in addition, that many Americans were losing confidence in a British government that refused to recognize the necessity of change. It "is truly discouraging to a people," he lamented, "who . . . by their dutiful behaviour during these times of American confusion have recommended themselves to the crown," to have "honorable and beneficial" requests for reform "so much neglected." Without reform ambitious sorts in America might be alienated from the parent state. "A Strange Government this," he grumbled, "in which Loyalty and Affection to the Sovereign is made Criminal, while a Servile Submission and Implicit Obedience to the Unjust and Oppressive Measures of a Private Subject is the only path to promotion."[15]

Galloway believed, furthermore, that deficiencies—even illegalities— in the colonial charters constituted just as serious an imperial defect as improper parliamentary taxes. Even though Galloway had contended that monarchs could never create communities independent of the sovereign government, he was forced to acknowledge that the colonial charters had been unwisely broad in their grants of power. He refused to concede that the charters had in fact created independent American governments, but he alleged that they created a condition which could logically culminate in American independence. The worst defect which he found in the charters was the failure to establish inferior polities which were modeled upon the government of the parent state. The colonial governments did not satisfactorily "harmonize with the system to which they belong," nor did they adequately emphasize the "supreme direction" of Parliament. Once Anglo-American hostilities had begun, he even maintained that the charters were "illegal and unconstitutional" because they so ineffectively stated the necessity for colonial subjugation to the British government.[16]

Galloway thought royal governments—those states with a crown-appointed executive and council, and an elected assembly—made the most ideal provincial government. But even this form of government might contain unsatisfactory aspects. If the governor and council were weak as they were in New England, the entire system would be devoid of adequate checks and balances. Then, instead of drawing support from the crown, the governor would become dependent on the very people "whose licentiousness he is appointed to check." Moreover, the councils in the New England colonies were selected by the legislatures from the "common rank of people" and were without dignity or distinction. Where aristocratic participation was wanting in government, Galloway asserted, a struggle was likely to develop between the governor and the assembly. In such an event the council surely would fail. Instead of acting as a bulwark against democracy, the council inevitably would be complaisant to the commons "whence *it receives its existence, and which may take it away at its pleasure.*" Furthermore, the assembly, through its control of the purse, had an effective weapon against the governor. Mixed government thus had been illusory in the royal colonies. Real power was vested in the democratic branch, an occurrence which propelled these colonies into the arms of those given to republican sentiment.[17]

Galloway did not doubt that the corporate colonies were the most unsavory of colonial governments. These polities, he thought, unleashed republicanism through each branch. With an elected executive, council, and legislature, these colonies inevitably became "the most ungovernable and licentious, and too often the scene of groundless discontent, faction and tumult."[18]

Galloway was most concerned with the proprietary form of government. He felt this form was "not warranted by the laws of *England*" and that "*no such Absurdity* and Inconveniency was ever *allowed*" under the British constitution. Several evils resulted from such a government. The proprietors, he charged, held too much power and more often than not were motivated solely by financial interests. The proprietors were not only not bound by a fixed tenure, but the checks imposed upon them in the charters were "nugatory, ineffectual, contradictory and absurd." In Maryland and Pennsylvania the proprietor had unavoidably become "an independent sovereign." Proprietary rule therefore altered the constitution by permitting the strengthening of executive powers at the expense of the other branches.

Such an aberration, exactly the opposite of the ills plaguing the royal and corporate colonies, developed because the Assembly was incapable of maintaining economic checks on an executive drawing most of his revenue from his extensive private estates. Furthermore, Pennsylvania's judges, often the appointees of the proprietors, were made subservient by their lack of independence. These captive judges were characterized by Galloway as "Sons of Oppression."[19]

The evils arising from proprietary rule, he concluded, led to a breakdown in patriotism and stimulated restlessness and rebellion. Moreover, because the government was so weak, the disorders could not be crushed. The accumulation of "injustice, ambition and oppression" destroyed the ability of government to protect its citizens and negated the real reason for the government to exist.[20]

Galloway did not disagree with even the most vitriolic colonial dissenter that America had serious grievances against the parent state. Nor could he discover the "least spark of reason" to demonstrate why the colonists should enjoy fewer rights than the inhabitants of Britain. After all, Englishmen had migrated to America with the consent of the government and pursued activities which increased the wealth and power of the empire. And he asked whether those "freemen in *England*" who immigrated had "become slaves by a six-weeks voyage to America." "Was the blood of your ancestors polluted by a change of soil?" Were Americans entitled to only a "tenth, an hundreth, or a thousandth" of the rights of Englishmen? If so, who would decide "your pittance, your short allowance . . . "?[21]

Galloway was an imperial patriot as well as a conservative statesman who labored tirelessly for imperial reform. This aspect of his career was less paradoxical than it might seem at first glance. Galloway was the heir to two powerful intellectual forces which influenced America during the century prior to the Revolution. Since the seventeenth century, strong currents of imperial nationalism, an intense devotion to the British empire and to the Anglo-American relationship, had flowed through the colonies. But a desire to reconstruct the empire had simultaneously existed on both sides of the Atlantic. Galloway espoused both ideals long before the colonial impasse occurred.

The loyalists in the Revolution—and Galloway, as a major spokesman for that cause—represented the last American exponents of Anglo-American nationalism. This concept of duel nationalism was based on the assumption that Great Britain and the colonies needed one another in order to flourish and to maintain social and political stability. It was natural for Americans to be patriotic toward the empire. Imperial policies affected the daily lives of many colonists, and for the most part the effects were favorable before 1765. Moreover, a vast literature, whose lineage reached from Sir

Walter Raleigh and Richard Hakluyt in the sixteenth century to Daniel Defoe and Henry, Viscount Bolingbroke in the eighteenth century, had instilled the notion that the empire exuded virtues for colonies and parent state alike. To a considerable degree these feelings were influenced by the real or imagined threats which Englishmen and colonists thought were facing the empire. Patriotism began with the assumption that the imperial union must be maintained to ensure English and American economic prosperity. America was portrayed as "a prodigy of wealth, immeasurable in its quantity, inexpressible in its value." But throughout the eighteenth century America was thought to be imperiled by France; if the colonies were lost, the imperialists asserted, the British way of life would be jeopardized. Before the 1760s few colonists would have maintained that the English way of life did not merit saving, and many believed that a brillant future of expansionism and profit awaited the empire. Through the combined efforts of Britain, already the world's strongest naval power, and America, the burgeoning, uncorrupted young continent, an empire of unparalleled plenty and power would be built.[22]

Many writers, however, believed the empire required substantial alteration before it could reach its full potential. Late in the previous century imperial nationalists had discovered weaknesses in the empire and had promoted a variety of solutions. The authors of these plans included American officials and proprietors as well as imperial functionaries in London. Several plans urged increased colonial cooperation through the creation of an American congress and a crown-appointed colonial executive. The revitalized structure, it was generally agreed, should enhance colonial military might and preserve the empire. None of the plans challenged English sovereignty and none advocated that the proposed colonial legislature usurp parliamentary power. One plan of the seventeenth century offered much more than a simple military union and, as a result, more nearly resembled Galloway's concepts than the others. In 1698 *An Essay Upon the Government of the English Plantations* appeared, probably written by Robert Beverley of Virginia. Beverley contemplated the limits of English jurisdiction as well as the existence of fundamental American rights which, he thought, could not be violated. He recognized serious weaknesses in the internal structure of the empire and, to correct the defects, advocated that all colonies be royalized and that all judges be appointed for life tenure. He also recommended a system by which Americans could check British intentions and hence offset London's monopolistic control of policy planning.[23]

By the time Galloway began to formulate his imperial theories, the literary world was witnessing a deluge of speculation on how the empire might best be reformed. This literature was sparked by the shocking administrative inefficiency which had occurred during the French and Indian

War, as well as by the breach between mother country and colonies which grew during the Stamp Act furor. All these writers began with the assumption that the empire was worth salvaging. Arthur Young, an Englishman better known for his agricultural experiments than his political theories, sounded the keynote. He argued that someday America would be so "absolutely invulnerable and universal" that it would be the protector of England; hence it was in England's interest to maintain the union, a task which could best be accomplished by ending the repression of America. This repression could be ended, Young maintained, by admitting eighty-six colonial representatives to Parliament. During the Stamp Act crisis Thomas Crowley advocated American home rule with Parliament managing only defensive concerns. At the same time another Englishman, Joshua Steele, proposed the creation of a council which would include colonists and non-colonists to direct American affairs. Francis Masères shortly thereafter urged that eighty colonists be admitted to Parliament, that one year elapse between the first and second readings of all bills pertaining to the colonies, and that all purely internal American affairs be left to the direction of the colonists.[24]

Three individuals exerted perhaps the greatest influence on Galloway. Thomas Pownall and Sir Francis Bernard, both senior imperial officials, produced highly publicized accounts of the American condition with thoughtful suggestions for remodeling the imperial relationship. Galloway's mentor Franklin, meanwhile, presented the most noteworthy reform plan in the colonies during the eighteenth century.

In 1764 Pownall, who had refused the governorship of Pennsylvania after serving as chief executive in Massachusetts, wrote *The Administration of the Colonies*. The tract went through six editions over the next thirteen years. Pownall believed the union could best function as a rather loosely governed "GRAND MARITIME DOMINION," but to accomplish this the central imperial government required reorganization. Although he acknowledged the need to maintain the political rights of the colonies, his primary contention was that the reforms would benefit the colonists economically.[25]

Bernard, a former governor of New Jersey and Massachusetts, penned his suggested remedies in the form of ninety-seven enumerated proposals. He assumed that historically Britain's rule of America had been poor because it "has been hitherto governed by temporary expedients." He advocated central rule with sovereign imperial power located in the British government, which was a composite of all its branches. The empire, he argued in a sentence Galloway often borrowed, could continue "no otherwise than by a subordination of the Colonies as *Dependent* states, to Great Britain as the *Imperial* sovereign. *Imperium in imperio* is a monster in politics which cannot subsist." He felt the rights of Americans must be protected. It was "most advisable to leave to the Provincial Legislatures the raising [of] the internal taxes"; Parliament, he thought, should intervene only when the colonies obstinately refused to act. He did not believe that American rights would be violated if Americans were subjected to taxes passed by a Parliament in which the colonists were not represented. This was the greatest difference in Bernard's and Galloway's viewpoints. Bernard stressed that a league of the colonies was desirable; dividing the colonies, he warned, "weakens the governing power, and strengthens that of the people; and thereby makes revolting more probable and more practicable." While permitting the colonists to unite, Bernard advocated governmental reform with the intention of making each provincial government larger and establishing a better balance between the various branches than presently existed. He urged that all governors be appointed by the crown and that they be made financially independent of the legislatures. Furthermore, he hoped that the members of the upper branch of the provincial assemblies would be drawn from a titled colonial nobility. This would provide the colonists with a "real and distinct third legislative power mediating between" the executive and the people. The lower house, he recommended, should be elected by the colonists. Each colony, thenceforth, would possess a genuinely balanced government.[26]

Franklin was the primary American exponent of imperial reform in the years immediately preceding the Revolution. The loquacious old sage unquestionably exerted a profound influence on Galloway. At the heart of Franklin's ideology were considerations of America's security and expansion, goals which until the late 1760s he believed could be realized only through close ties with Britain. Britain would provide arms to shield the colonists from other expansionists while acting as an umpire to subdue intracolonial disputes. Only British arms, Franklin exhorted, could conquer the trans-Appalachian belt, a region essential to the welfare of the colonies since it could act as living space for the swelling American population. Franklin suggested that in a century the American population would be greater than that of England. "What an accession of power to the British empire by sea as well as land," he concluded. "What increase of trade and navigation; What numbers of ships and seamen!" He believed the colonists could strengthen their security by forming an American union, but before imperial relations soured it was the Anglo-American union which most interested Franklin. Britain, he assured a member of the Assembly Party, "is the Safety as well as [the] Honour of the Colonies." He hoped "that by such a union, the people of Great Britain, and the people of the colonies, would learn to consider themselves, as not belonging to different interests, but to one community with one interest; which I imagine would contribute to strengthen the whole."[27] Galloway never wavered from Franklin's teachings. On the one hand, he repeatedly alluded to the immediate security Britain could provide the helpless colonists; on the other hand, he dreamed of the limitless power future generations would possess.

Franklin also believed that greater American unity would facilitate the growth of imperial power. In 1754 he and several other colonial leaders presented unification plans at the Albany Conference. His plan was similar to many of those presented during the previous century, but it fell considerably short of Galloway's later, more daring proposal. Consequently, the contents of the plan had less influence on Galloway than many contemporaries and historians have realized. The American structure which Franklin advocated was akin to that envisioned by Galloway. The colonies would have been governed by a crown-appointed executive and a national congress chosen by the colonists. However, these officials would have existed primarily to confront military problems. Franklin skirted the thorny problem of sovereignty on nonmartial matters. The most notable influence of the Albany Plan on Galloway was simply that a plan had been introduced by a colonist, thus perpetuating a tradition which had endured for nearly half a century.[28]

Galloway remained a steadfast imperial patriot throughout his career. He was convinced that Great Britain possessed the world's most enlightened government—to "be a subject of Great Britain," he observed, "is to be the freest subject of any civil community anywhere to be found on earth." He believed that it was because of the empire that Americans were able to enjoy "the *rights*, *liberties* and *freedom*, of the *most free state* upon earth."[29]

He was convinced that the interests of England and America were inseparable. He concluded that "their Happiness, their Dignity and Reputation among other Nations with their common Safety, depend upon a solid political Union." Because of the great similarity in "their Laws and Language, Trade and Commerce and, above all . . . the Protestant Religion," he questioned whether it was "possible for one to subsist without the other." Until America grew strong British protection was essential both in forestalling foreign threats and in preventing a lapse into an American civil war. Moreover, through the beneficence and security provided by Britain, America had become a land "where agriculture . . . philosophy, and all the liberal arts and sciences have been nourished and ripened to a degree of perfection, astonishing to mankind . . . and where freedom, peace and order, have always triumphed."[30]

He dreamed grandiosely of colonial expansion, but he still conceived of westward adventure as a joint British-American enterprise. Like his adversaries, Galloway thought of America as an extraordinary continent.

Considering its current weaknesses, however, he thought the continent's uniqueness would be in greater peril, at least for the next several generations, if Americans deserted the empire.[31]

In Galloway's opinion the empire was equally essential to the well-being of Great Britain. Should America be lost to the empire, British power would be greatly diminished. The colonies were the "nursery" of the empire's seamen and the producer of raw materials essential for its naval stores. Britain's commerce with America would languish. Imperial intercourse, he insisted, was much less difficult to arrange than trade between two sovereign nations. In the empire trade "depends not on the changes or caprice of foreign councils, not upon the intrigues of our enemies, nor upon the alteration of the circumstances of a country. It is *our own.*" In short, "one *grand and illustrious Empire*" would ensure "the *best of all political securities against the future.*" Galloway remained one of America's last great defenders of the old patriotism. Whereas years before Franklin had boasted, "I am a Briton," Galloway could still, at a much later date, assert with arrogance, "We must therefore, *like Englishmen*, exert our power."[32]

Despite Galloway's undiluted devotion to Britain, he acknowledged the need to reconstitute the empire. But he did not deceive himself that the reforms he offered would entirely eradicate all friction between the colonists and the parent state. Bad feeling was certain to persist, he feared, from unavoidable mercantile restrictions. He also suspected that the empire would continue to be jeopardized by vicious plotters. There would always be conspirators in London willing to foment "conflagration and massacre" in America so that a ministry might be toppled, and he knew that every empire contained malcontents who worked for colonial independence. In addition, the extreme distance between America and Great Britain would cause dissension. Petty grievances might blossom into real problems before colonial administrators could receive instructions from London. America's "distance from the Seat of Empire" therefore made it imperative that the imperial partners establish a perfect governmental structure. He even conceded that American independence was likely in the remote future. The distance of the colonies from the parent country might ultimately weaken national affections and prompt the colonists to question the strength of Britain. When the colonists awakened to these sentiments they would promptly "throw off their Subordination."[33]

Galloway was under no delusions, however, that geography was responsible for the imperial conflict. The "distance of a Member of the Politic Body," he suggested, "has as little to do with the good or ill Government of it, or with its Obedience to the supreme Authority, as that of a Member of the human Body which, however distant or near, equally obeys the human will." The dilemma which confronted Britain and her colonies was of a constitutional nature, and its resolution—he was convinced—required the reconciliation of the liberty of the colonists to the authority of the imperial government.[34]

It has been argued that Galloway was destroyed as an American politician because of his inability to reconcile America's lack of representation in Parliament with the means, as a subordinate community, of seeking redress for America's real or fancied grievances. The failure to attain redress of grievances plagued conservatives as well as radicals, and ultimately led to expedients such as the economic boycotts which escalated the quarrel. However, the real problem which confronted Galloway was to discover a settlement which would provide an adequate representation of America while preserving the imperial sovereignty of the Parliament.[35]

Galloway realized that many types of imperial union were possible, but by 1774 three configurations had attracted the most attention in the colonies. A majority at the First Continental Congress probably desired some form of commonwealth. In such a union the empire would be united by a sovereign executive but there would be no common legislature. The monarch would exercise certain prerogative powers and all legislative powers would be reserved to the assembly of each member nation. Before 1776 John Adams, Thomas Jefferson, James Wilson, and Richard Bland, among others, generally favored an empire structured in such a manner. A second form of polity—a federal structure—was also championed. In a union of this type a sovereign central government would rule the empire. But the government of Britain would be subordinated to the level of the other member states, and each polity would be afforded representation in the central government. At times both James Otis and Benjamin Franklin sought to reconstruct the empire along these lines. The British government offered a third style of imperial polity. The sovereign government would have remained essentially unchanged under this scheme, although imperial powers would be formally acknowledged, clarified, and utilized.[36]

Galloway expressed reservations about each proposed change. He regarded the commonwealth ideal as an absurdity. Every union, he thought, required a central legislative branch. Furthermore, he believed such a union was "merely founded in a commercial treaty" and would soon be too emasculated to endure. "We must not . . . rely on a Commercial connection without a just system of polity to retain it," he counseled. Galloway objected to the federal structure because it would effectively deny the parent state a veto over the colonies. He disparaged the kind of imperial structure recommended by the ministry because the internal structure of the colonies would be left intact, thus permitting a continuance of the "licentiousness" and "democracy" which he believed had caused the maladies in

THE LOYALIST MIND

the existing governments. Such a union, moreover, would not calm the objections of the colonial dissenters.[37]

Although Galloway was influenced by the intellectual currents of the age, his conception of imperial reform was unique. Under the plans he contrived the colonists would have shared in the imperial legislative powers, yet remained subordinate to the authority of Great Britain. His plans came closer to approximating the federal design which the United States created in the late 1780s than did any other reform scheme suggested during the period of revolutionary turmoil. The logic upon which his plans were predicated, in fact, was often strikingly similar to that manifested in *The Federalist.*

Although Galloway offered several plans, a consistent strain runs throughout, and the designs contain only slight variations. His initial plan—which was formulated during the Stamp Act upheaval in 1765, but was never formally presented—has been lost. The first plan to be tendered and published was the scheme he presented to the First Continental Congress. During the Revolution he drafted plans for Lord Germain and Charles Jenkinson, Lord North's secretary at war. Following the Treaty of Paris he conceived an additional plan.[38]

The vital element in Galloway's plan for imperial reconciliation—a plan he recommended in nearly every pamphlet he wrote after 1774 and which he suggested during his examination by the Commons in 1779—was the proposal for the establishment of a bicameral American Congress to serve as the "fourth branch of the British Legislature." Since a governmental union could be maintained only by the "*Joint assent*" of all its parts, it was necessary either to admit colonial representatives to the Commons or to create an American branch of Parliament. He preferred the first alternative, but American leaders were so cool to the idea that Galloway felt compelled to propose the creation of the "new Branch." The establishment of another house of Parliament would not be unique, he contended, since, in the Middle Ages, the creation of the House of Commons itself had merely been an act of expediency. Moreover, the "new Branch" was compatible with the concept of balances. In this case, however, imperial equilibrium was sought through balancing American interests against British interest. Like Madison's famous defense of the Constitution in the tenth *Federalist*, Galloway's work suggested that a balanced polity encompassing a broad territorial expanse would be stable and the dangers of factionalism—majority faction versus the minority, imperial interest versus the colonial interest—would be diminished. His "new Branch" would, however, mirror the existing branches of Parliament only so far as questions of the empire were concerned. Otherwise, it was to be inferior to the established houses. He realized that the proposed system would not be absolutely perfect; the jurisdiction of the American branch would not extend to British affairs, although

Britain would possess an independent legislature and the power to exercise some dominion over America.[39]

Galloway's proposed branch was to consist of an executive—whom he sometimes titled the "President General" and at other times the "Lord-Lieutenant"—and an assembly which he referred to as the "Grand Council." In all his plans the executive was to be appointed by the crown and serve at royal pleasure. Initially he called for a unicameral legislative branch, but in later plans he recommended that the assembly be of a bicameral nature. The upper house, the Council, was to serve as both the cabinet of advisors to the executive and as a legislative body. In his later schemes he, like Bernard, openly suggested that the members of this upper chamber be "vested with some degree of rank and dignity above the Commons." He recommended that these councillors be given the status of noblemen and be granted the title of "Baron." Men of such stature, he believed, would think twice before succumbing to rebellious spirits. Having derived "all their Rank, Dignity, Power and Importance, from the Crown," only madmen would contend for a "dissolution of the Connection." Upon independence they would find themselves "reduced from superior Eminence and Dignity in Life to a level with the populace." The members of the Council were to be appointed by the crown and serve life terms unless removed by the united action of the executive officer and the lower house. Galloway viewed the lower house as the representative of the people, and his concept of this body changed little from plan to plan. The members of this house, he thought, should be elected by all the provincial assemblies on the American mainland—that is, the original thirteen mainland colonies as well as the newer British colonies in the Floridas and Canada—for three-year terms. The "Grand Council" was to meet annually.[40]

If structured in this manner, the principles which characterized the British government would typify the subordinate government. The "American Branch" would be "*in Miniature* a perfect resemblance of the Principal Government." The government of the colonial union would, additionally, be a government of branches "so tempered and mixed together" that it would naturally coexist with the other elements of the central imperial polity.[41]

However it was to be constituted, the American government was created to regulate American affairs and was to be "considered as an inferior Branch of the British Legislature." The Assembly's unilateral jurisdiction was to extend only to the police powers customarily exercised by subordinate units, and, even then, all legislative enactments of the "new Branch" were to be subject to the assent of both Parliament and the American executive. This would prevent colonial legislation from becoming law without British assent, a condition which might provoke "sedition, disloyalty, and infringement of the King's prerogative." By the same token, all parliamentary bills pertaining to America would take effect only after approval by the colonial branch. Galloway would have permitted the assembly to be called into session or adjourned and dissolved by either the colonial executive or the monarch, but in any event it was to be allowed to meet at least once each year.[42]

Galloway hoped to devise a system that would provide adequate imperial revenue without violating the colonists' rights as Englishmen. He proposed that in times of peace, Parliament—including the American branch—establish fixed quotas for each colony, which could then be assessed as each provincial assembly decreed. During times of war the crown should be permitted arbitrarily to collect American revenues; his plan, however, contained no provision which stated that America would have a voice in the declaration of war. He also suggested that the colonies be allowed their own currency in order to purchase goods manufactured in Britain, and he insisted that colonists be allowed the same mercantile and manufacturing privileges enjoyed by the citizens of Great Britain. While he would have allowed Britain to place tariff duties on the importation of competitive colonial goods, he would not have extended reciprocal powers to the colonists.[43]

With each proposal Galloway added new elements to his plan. For example, he once urged the repeal of all parliamentary legislation inconsistent with the principles of his proposed union. In later plans he frequently recommended that American commissioners be allowed to sit in Parliament. These commissioners were to be denied voting rights, but would be allowed to act as observors and join in the debates. Despite his involvement in the anti-proprietary struggle in Pennsylvania, Galloway did not urge the First Continental Congress to consider royal control of all colonies. He acted pragmatically, for the introduction of such a matter would only have made reconciliation more difficult to achieve. Once the Revolution began, however, Galloway quickly became a public advocate for a uniform style of colonial organizations. He recommended that all colonial governments should consist of a governor and privy council appointed by the crown. Both would have served at royal pleasure. The executive wing of these governments would be counterbalanced by the bicameral assemblies. The members of the privy councils would act as the upper legislative chambers. The members of the lower houses would be popularly elected for specified terms. In addition, he urged that all colonial judges, revenue-collectors, and military officials be appointed by and serve at the discretion of the crown. This overhaul of colonial governments would "root out the seeds of disaffection and rebellion." Inferior governments similar in structure to the sovereign polity would lead to "one People of the same Mind" in all parts of the empire. Reform, he contended, would bring Britain into the modern world since she was the only major power which permitted subordinate units to have forms of governance at variance with that of the sovereign state. Once reform was enacted the colonists would be capable of satisfactorily meeting their obligations. Then "Britain can have in Justice no further pecuniary demands on them as Members of her Society."[44]

Galloway also proposed a variety of measures designed to inhibit provincial malcontents. He recommended that the crown appoint two Anglican bishops for America, and he hoped that clergymen would have a salutary impact on colonial public opinion and on the intellectual atmosphere. Although he publicly urged "full liberty of Conscience," he hoped the teachings of the Anglicans would undermine the influences exerted by the Puritan-related churchmen and advocated that the state closely regulate all ecclesiastical meetings and synods to ascertain their loyalty and propriety. As an additional safeguard against republican excesses in the colonies, Galloway urged the curtailment of town meetings. He regarded these meetings as the source of considerable evil and believed they should be permitted only when sanctioned by legitimate government authorities.[45]

As a final protection against the growth of popular power in America, Galloway advocated that the salaries of all executive and judicial officials in the colonies be "ascertained and fixed" in Great Britain. Under this plan the chief American executive would draw a salary from monies concurrently provided by all the colonies in the union. The provincial officials would be compensated through revenue raised in each colony. Galloway frankly believed that a governor assured of a fixed salary "would be more attentive to his duty, and more firm in his opposition to popular claims." To permit the colonies to continue appropriating gubernatorial salaries would be to weaken the "Authority and influence of the Crown, and strengthen . . . the Power of the People, so as to destroy that balance of Power which is the great Security of a Mixt form of Government." Such changes in the internal political affairs of the colonies, he added, would cause Great Britain to be "more attentive to and watchful over the Conduct of the Colonies than heretofore."[46]

In the final analysis the stability of the empire depended on a sound constitutional foundation and the loyalty of the American masses. In a world quickening to the call of nationalism, Galloway realized that Anglo-American patriotism would be difficult to maintain. His solution was to advocate a rigorous dose of imperial indoctrination for the colonists. He assumed that it was "education alone which forms and fixes human habits, manners, attachments, and aversions. . . . So men, educated in the principles of one form of government, will ever esteem and prefer it." When the laws were uniform throughout the empire they would be "lessons of instruction, by which every subject is daily taught his duty and mode of obedience to the State."[47]

THE LOYALIST MIND

In short, Galloway argued,

Train them up, when in their infancy, in those principles, which will teach them to love the Parent State; give them the same constitutional subordination; govern them by the same measure of power; and let them enjoy the same measure of liberty as the citizens and other subjects enjoy; and they will not, because they can have no motive to, depart from the obedience. Do this and they will ever love and respect the Parent State, whose protection never ceases, and from which they are daily receiving every blessing. Do this, and their particular and local "pride and violence" will be changed into national attachment; and their impatience of restraint be only a visionary notion, because that restraint will be imposed by their own consents, and become their own act, to which they will readily submit. I say, do this, and the American Colonies . . . will, as the Roman Colonies did . . . adhere to the State.[48]

The irony of Galloway's career was that while contemporaries regarded his views as anachronistic, he had, in fact, reached an understanding of political theory that in many respects bore a striking resemblance to the point of view later championed by the Founding Fathers in the 1780s. But Galloway's dilemma was vastly dissimilar to that encountered by the Federalists. Galloway was a royalist who attempted to preserve a political union challenged by an armed revolt, whereas the Federalists were republicans who attempted to establish a union insulated from the conflicts which inevitably troubled human affairs. Both Galloway and the Federalists thought it essential that every polity have a central government with an unquestioned claim to sovereignty. Both thought it necessary that local entities—colonies in the one instance, states in the other—be represented in the sovereign central legislature; both thought these inferior governments must retain some measure of local autonomy. Each recommended a similar solution to the revenue-raising question—that thorniest of problems within the Anglo-American relationship as well as during the Articles of Confederation era. Both favored a balanced government concept. Neither cared much for the direct election of officials, both limiting this procedure to one house in a bicameral assembly. Each sought to make judges independent of the other agencies of government. Both believed inferior governments should be modeled upon the sovereign government. Finally, both were troubled by the prospect of upheaval and social dislocation, and both believed dissidence would be contained as the extent of the domain was enlarged.

Galloway was aware that his plans were not without fault, but he believed they would correct most of the ills of the empire and aid in establishing a perpetual union between the parent state and the colonies. The dilemma he faced during the imperial crisis was that of finding a means to somehow reconcile the violated colonial liberties with the necessity to maintain British sovereignty. The solution he recommended reflected his political ideology and was structured about his ideal tenets of sovereignty and balanced government. Strife was at the heart of Galloway's ideology: struggle between men; struggle between the branches in any government; struggle between the sovereign and subordinate governments. Galloway did not delude himself that his schemes would eliminate conflict. Discord was endemic to man and his institutions. But he was confident that his plans, based as they were on the enlightened concepts of men as diverse as Hobbes and the Real Whigs, Franklin and Bernard, Burlamaqui and Blackstone, offered a reasonable opportunity to secure peace and promote domestic tranquillity. In pursuit of that end he was willing to recommend an enormous overhaul of the empire and to risk—and ultimately to ruin—his career.

5

The Historian:

"To nourish the seeds of American sedition"

Shortly after the Revolution a flood of historical accounts appeared. Although participants on both sides contributed to the swelling literature, only a few loyalists published their versions of those turbulent years. As Bernard Bailyn noted recently, no Tory panegyric was forthcoming as a "heroic counterinterpretation" to the "unqualified heroics" of the nationalistic histories produced by the likes of Parson Weems and David Ramsay. Some of the more articulate loyalists, of course, used the idleness imposed by exile to probe the rebellion; generally, however, the expatriates were unwilling to make their views public. "They wrote," Bailyn observed, "but they kept their writing private, and left it to posterity to vindicate the choice they had so fatally made."[1]

Galloway was not one of the reticent exiles. In 1780 he published a lengthy survey of the causes of the Revolution under the title *Historical and Political Reflections on the Rise and Progress of the American Rebellion*, as well as a military history of the upheaval entitled *An Account of the Conduct of the War in the Middle Colonies*. Both inquiries were published as part of the pamphleteering which enlivened London as the war grew progressively more hopeless for Great Britain. Neither pamphlet caused much comment at the time, and neither was of consequence in historical literature.

Yet the histories reveal something of Joseph Galloway. As always, they not only divulge information about the era under scrutiny but provide insights about the author and the period in which the study was written. They open still another view of his loyalist mind and behavior.

Galloway saw certain utilitarian virtues in the study of history. The state, like the human body, was inevitably "liable to disorders, which often

terminate in death." If attended by a "physical quack"—an inept administration—the patient would be subjugated to "agonies and convulsions"
followed by death. Galloway therefore implored Englishmen to scrutinize
the origins of the rebellion. From a study of the Revolution the ministers
might find the clue to its "immediate suppression, and from this alone can
that system of future policy be formed, which can effect a permanent
union . . . and prevent another rebellion."[2]

Galloway's appraisal of the Revolution was a sophisticated contemporary account. He rejected the allegations of the "malcontents on both
sides" who charged that Britain was solely to blame for the upheaval. The
Americans emphasized British culpability in order to justify their treasonous behavior; the opposition in Britain "echoed it, some of them to conceal
their thirst for the emoluments and dignities of office, the sole ground of
their opposition," and others because they sympathized with the republican
ideology espoused by colonial radicals. While Galloway repudiated Britain's
sole responsibility for the rebellion, he did not consider the parent state
entirely blameless. He found its activities wanting in certain vital respects.
He laid most of the blame at the feet of colonial agitators, but he forcefully
uncovered deep roots for the turmoil, roots which had made it possible for
the agitators to flourish.[3]

To the loyalists the American Rovolution was a curious, mystifying
event. Unrest, they believed, normally occurred in the wake of a "continued
series of extreme injustice and oppression in the rulers." In such an environment demagogues found it easy "to incite the vulgar and ignorant to sedition, and finally to throw off their allegiance" to the legitimate government.
But the colonial rebellion occurred in a dissimilar setting, Galloway argued.
Neither "antecedent injustice nor oppression" abounded on the colonial
landscape. When hostilities erupted the colonists were "more free, unen-
cumbered and happy" than any other peoples. Great Britain had nourished
the colonies in infancy and supported them in adulthood; it had encouraged
the colonial economy through generous bounties, and it had repeatedly
pacified Indians maligned by colonial "acts of fraud and injustice." If the
colonies were attacked by a foreign state, Great Britain had "not failed to
resent the injury." The "treasure and blood of Britons have been devoted to
[the colonists'] preservation." In the French and Indian War Britain had, in
fact, "saved them from ruin" and magnanimously permitted the colonists to
contribute to the conflict as they pleased.[4]

Historically, Galloway thought, imperial problems arose because of
the heavy-handed and oppressive policies of the parent state. Rome, "proud
and insolent," had permitted its colonists insufficient freedoms. But Britain,
except to placate its frequently lamenting colonists, paid little attention to
America before 1763. "Thus," he concluded, "Rome and Britain wan-

dered . . . in different and opposite extremes; extremes which naturally produced the same effects, the revolt of their Colonies."[5]

The histories contended that the "Seeds of [the] American Rebellion have been . . . long planted, long in vegetation." Galloway maintained that dissatisfaction with Britain "first broke out" in those colonies "formed on principles the most variant from" those of the parent state. Hence, the New England colonies, with their peculiar charter polities, took the initiative in goading for independence. Three forces propelled New England toward its treasonable conduct. Republican government, he wrote, was so unavoidably contentious and discordant as to make the calamity of rebellion inevitable. Moreover, the republican nature of these societies blinded the ignorant masses to the virtues of the British system, so that the administration's reform policies of the 1760s and 1770s were greeted with scorn. Finally, trained in republicanism, these colonists were steeled to resist—by violence, if necessary—any British attempt to alter their provincial governments.[6]

If a rebellion was the only means by which the inhabitants of the charter colonies could maintain their governments against the encroachments of England, many residents of Pennsylvania, he thought, saw the rebellion as an opportunity to end the evils of proprietary government. Galloway believed this was a confirmation, not a contradiction, of his maxim that people remained loyal to the government under which they had been raised. He believed the proprietors in the eighteenth century had forsaken William Penn's original frame of government and had broken the original covenant with the governed. Pennsylvania's government had become a tyranny from which its residents hoped to escape. Even before hostilities began Galloway had insisted that the British refusal to allay proprietary despotism was driving loyal Pennsylvanians into the arms of radical demagogues. He complained to Franklin as early as 1765 that because the "royal ear" was closed on the proprietary issue many were driven to "disorder and confusion."[7]

Even the proprietors hoped for independence, Galloway had claimed falsely. In 1783 he reiterated these charges. The increase in proprietary wealth and power, he claimed, "naturally produced their ambition" for additional strength until "nothing less than perfect independence of the British Government could satisfy it." Not content with being "the most wealthy subjects in the British dominions," the proprietors "wished to become perfect and absolute independent Princes." However, the proprietors were so subtle, according to Galloway, that few people perceived that they were really revolutionaries. The proprietors had little to fear in attempting to secure independence. If separation from Britain was accomplished, Pennsylvania, in the estimation of Galloway, would remain under proprietary rule because the Penn family's closest allies—men like John Dickinson and

Charles Thomson—were also revolutionaries. If the revolt for independence failed, the proprietors were equally secure for their true intentions were sufficiently disguised to delude both the ministry and most loyalists. Hence, Galloway maintained, when opposition to the Stamp Act surfaced in 1765, the proprietors were the "abettors and promoters of sedition." However, when the proprietors finally awakened to the dangers of the situation in 1775 and realized that a successful revolution would sweep aside their rule as well as that of Britain, they allied with the loyalists. By then, however, the government was too weak and unpopular to halt the revolutionaries.[8]

It was not just the blemished provincial governments which made the rebellion likely. The nature of the people living in New England made some form of Anglo-American discord inevitable according to Galloway. The region was settled in the seventeenth century by Puritans—a species whose "principles of ecclesiastical polity was as directly repugnant to those of the established church, as their ideas of civil government were to those of a mixed monarchy." Such a people, he conjectured, would never make "good and faithful subjects to a state" because they believed "the right to all *civil* as well as *ecclesiastical* power originated in the people." Once in Massachusetts the Puritans vested the powers of "direction and punishment, in all cases whatsoever, in the people at large." Their first charter was "merely republican" and conformed to their "democratical wishes and principles." Galloway charged that the charter of 1628 was illegal, an "intolerable" grant which had produced repeated "mischiefs to the peace." No British monarch ever held the power to permit the lower house of a colonial assembly to share in the appointment of the upper branch of the legislature. Such an occurrence negated the "aristocratic part of the constitution" and rendered the executive helpless, a mere "cypher" before the assembly. Not even the charter of 1690 remedied the colony's afflicted polity. The new charter neither eradicated "the spirit of their Mosaical laws" nor checked the "licentious power of the people," so that over the years the colony had never hesitated to enact laws "totally repugnant . . . and subversive" to British policies. The diseased system only heightened Puritan dislike for all aspects of British culture and provoked an incessant history of "turbulent and seditious conduct." Puritan inclinations, moreover, merely aggravated the "Violent Temper of the Americans," a people of frontier primitivism.[9]

In light of New England's supposed nonconformity, how could Galloway explain a century and a half of Anglo-American peace? Radicals, he contended, had secretly plotted for independence from the beginning, but they were compelled to await the proper moment with "solicitude and impatience." For much of the time the colonists were in an infant state, "incompetent in numbers." The colonies, moreover, were divided and quarrelsome. The enormous immigration of peoples of dissimilar nationality and

THE LOYALIST MIND

ideology presented an additional problem. Warfare, however, more than any other eighteenth-century factor, kept the colonists "employed, harassed and distressed. The neighborhood of Canada, and the designs of France . . . were so many obstacles to their design." Events in the early 1760s removed the obstacles which had inhibited the radicals. By 1763 the Indian threat was controlled and France had surrendered its claims to North America. "Nothing was now wanting, but a plan for collecting their strength and uniting with those of similar inclinations."[10]

To colonial radicals, Galloway alleged, the passage of the Stamp Act in 1765 simply provided a pretext for action. The core of resistance came from "a small interested faction." The great majority of the colonists never wavered in their devotion to Great Britain. Galloway deduced several revolutionary elements which skulked about in an effort to inflame passions. Lawyers and merchants "who thought their professional business would be affected" by British actions frequently denounced controversial parliamentary legislation. Some urban artisans and yeomen farmers—the element he collectively labeled the "ignorant vulgar"—were, not surprisingly, misled by their social betters. Furthermore, he claimed, "bankrupt planters, who were overwhelmed in debt to their British factors," as well as "smuggling merchants in the sea-port towns" supported the rebellion from obvious economic motives. The malcontents, he added, profited from an excellent organization. The extremists had agents in each colony and remained in close contact through a network of couriers. Not only did the political leadership establish an efficient organization, but religious groups were even coordinated to aid the rebellion. New England Congregationalists were by nature troublemakers, he thought. To the south, Presbyterians formed a synod to spread seditious materials. Successful in this venture, the synod attempted to form a similar interdenominational structure.[11]

British insurgents, Galloway complained, also nurtured the rebellion. American independence was of secondary consideration to this mutinous cabal. These rebels hoped primarily that the growth of colonial discord would cause the ministry to collapse and would lead to the destruction of the monarchy and the democratization of the realm. The plotters were willing to resort to "conflagration and massacres" to attain their objectives, and these "seditious combinations" were in constant touch with American "spies" living in England. Franklin, he conjectured, was the leading light among the colonial espionage agents. According to Galloway, the English conspirators expected the ministry to collapse if threatened with a colonial revolt. Consequently, "the measures of sedition from time to time were concerted and transmitted, by this Faction in Britain," to the colonial revolutionaries. He charged, for example, that the schemes of nonimportation originated in Britain. The "seditious speeches in parliament, [the] petitions, pamphlets, and publications" of those in England who abetted the rebellion "would fill a volume in folio," he lamented. The friendship and aid extended the colonial republicans by their powerful counterparts in London had, in Galloway's estimation, an important psychological impact. With such friends, the rebellious Americans were encouraged to persist in their efforts.[12]

The British, Galloway charged, made four grievous blunders during these critical years. First, when the colonists were helpless and in desperate straits during the French and Indian War, the ministry should have imposed taxes on America. The colonists would have accepted the duties to survive, and the important precedent of parliamentary taxation would have been established. Moreover, the administration would have been fully justified in taxing America. The colonial population was a quarter that of the parent state, and its wealth swelled enormously during the conflict. Great Britain "contributed not a little to her opulence" by pumping "incredible sums" into America. Furthermore, while Britain suffered during the war American "freighted ships" sailed the globe—even trading covertly with Britain's enemies—and "returned loaded with treasure." But Britain, owing to faulty information, considered the colonists as infants; "lest it unwittingly impose burthens she was unable to sustain," the parent state shrank from placing too much pressure on her offspring.[13]

A second fundamental error committed by Britain, according to Galloway, was the decision to strip Canada from the beleaguered French in the Treaty of Paris. He attributed much of the blame for this lamentable decision to the advice offered by the esteemed but untrustworthy Franklin. He described his former partner as "a Bostonian by birth, a republican in principle, and a person of great intrigue and abilities." Galloway also acknowledged, however, that Great Britain acquired Canada because it could not depend on America for military assistance. Britain could have only gained by leaving Canada in the possession of France. So long as Franco-Spanish encirclement of the colonies remained practicable, he surmised, the colonists would have hesitated to sever their military-economic ties with Great Britain.[14]

Britain's third error, Galloway maintained, lay in the manner in which the ministry attempted to reform the empire. Galloway was certainly sympathetic with the idea of overhauling the structure, but he believed the planners should have "taken the Matter up a little deeper" and searched for "the most proper Plan for cementing the two Countries together upon such Principles of Government and Policy, as would have enabled them to obtain what they wanted." Had the ministers granted to "America the same Rights and Privileges as are enjoyed by the Subjects in Britain," the alterations would have been accomplished painlessly.[15]

THE LOYALIST MIND

Following the culmination of hostilities, Britain embarked on its policy of imperial taxation. Galloway thought the idea of assessing Americans was eminently fair and justified. The ministry, he argued, merely expected "an equal distribution of the burthens of society." Was Britain to tax three-fourths of its population and "permit the other fourth to be exempted"? Was the ministry to "suffer the opulence of America to increase, and her sons to riot in luxury and dissipation without contributing a reasonable proportion" to the imperial treasury? "Were Britons to become hewers of wood, and drawers of water, for an American faction?" Two factors necessitated the Stamp Act, he declared. The government was intent on providing an adequate national defense, and it insisted on an "equal distribution of the burthens necessary for the purpose."[16]

When the Stamp Act was greeted by a chorus of opposition in the colonies, Great Britain committed still another fatal blunder. The ministry repealed the legislation. This initial act of appeasement "tended to encourage and nourish the seeds of American sedition . . . now growing fast to a dangerous maturity." Had the government enforced the act until the colonists learned of its harmless nature, Galloway asserted, the rebellion would have been prevented "at least for the present." But the government was not finished with its surrender to the "groundless clamours" of the colonists. When the Declaratory Act was passed as an accompaniment to the repeal of the Stamp Act, the ministry hastened to alert the radicals that it had no intention of enforcing the legislation. Furthermore, four years later the Townshend Duties could have been sustained by "firmness" and "intrepidity of spirit," but the ministry again lost its nerve and repealed those taxes after a short trial.[17]

Galloway denied that the Tea Act of 1773 produced "universal alarm." The legislation upset those "attached to democratical principles," but the majority of Americans "rather approved than condemned the measure." The radicals, therefore, left "no art, no fraud, no falsehood" untouched in an effort to provoke hostilities. The New England zealots "set every engine at work." Some radicals insisted that Britain plotted to enslave the colonists, others attacked monarchical traditions or observed supposed examples of British corruption. Still others expressed the "flattering idea that '*America would soon become a great empire!*' " once it secured independence. How the Massachusetts radicals could openly and successfully fan the "flame of rebellion" in a province under the eye of His Majesty's army was a mystery to Galloway. Nevertheless, the radicals remained ineffective outside Massachusetts until Britain passed the Coercive Acts. Then the radicals had their "instrument to deceive and mislead the ignorant and incautious into rebellion."[18]

By the summer of 1774 the moderates, including Galloway, at last recognized that the "design and ultimate wish of the Bostonian faction and their British colleagues" was American independence. To forestall such an eventuality, many moderates urged the convocation of an American congress which might seek a *rapprochement* with Great Britain. The plan would have succeeded, Galloway acrimoniously charged, except for the "injudicious conduct" of several governors. These executives refused to permit their assemblies to select delegates, so that many congressmen were elected by "illegal and factious" rump legislatures. The number of radical delegates skyrocketed, and Congress, consequently, was of a most "motley complexion."[19]

Two factions struggled in the Congress. A moderate element "dutifully" sought to petition for redress and attain a "solid and constitutional union" with Great Britain. The radicals, who had secretly yearned for independence since before the Stamp Act, now threw aside all pretense. Through every imaginable "fiction, falsehood, and fraud" they attempted to "delude the people from their due allegiance, to throw the subsisting Governments into anarchy, to incite the ignorant and vulgar to arms." This radical faction, the loyalist said, was composed chiefly of "congregational and presbyterian republicans." Its leader was "Samuel Adams—a man, who though by no means remarkable for brilliant abilities, yet is equal to most men in popular intrigue, and the management of a faction. He eats little, drinks little, sleeps little, thinks much, and is most decisive and indefatigable in the pursuit of his objects."[20]

The congressional factions struggled equally for three weeks. Then Galloway introduced his plan of union. The fate of the rebellion, he proudly implied in his history, hung in the balance. But the radicals, now desperate, turned to terror tactics and "lessened the firmness of some of the loyalists"; by a narrow margin compromise was rejected. Having succeeded at last, the radicals rammed through an American Bill of Rights "calculated to incense and irritate . . . rather than to obtain a redress of grievances." Later that autumn the radicals commenced a trade embargo which was "carried into execution by every act of violence that lawless committees and desperate mobs could devise." Meanwhile, the loyalists were disarmed and removed from positions of authority.[21]

Even after a year of hostilities and "all the arts of intrigue," however, Congress remained "equally divided" between those desiring reconciliation and those favoring independence. By the summer of 1776 the military situation demanded foreign assistance; but a declaration of independence would have failed, Galloway alleged, had not John Dickinson, "a gentleman naturally timid and variable in his opinion, retracted his opinion, and gave the casting vote."[22]

Galloway depicted the history of Britain's conduct of the war as a deplorable spectacle. Inept and overly cautious commanders repeatedly

THE LOYALIST MIND

either permitted Washington's escape or lost entire armies to barely trained provincial officers. Britain committed error upon error. It did not adequately utilize the swarms of loyalists inhabiting the colonies. It employed outmoded strategy geared to an antiquated mode of warfare—the army's maneuvers were cumbersome and ill-founded. Its navy, despite overwhelming numerical superiority, was incompetent to fashion an effective blockade. Instead of holding and occupying important urban coastal centers, the administration pursued the unsound strategy of ineffectual forays through largely uninhabited terrain. The same traitorous group which had aided in fomenting the rebellion, Galloway charged, assisted the generals in losing the war. Their object remained the same as before the fighting—to topple the ministry and republicanize Britain's society and institutions.[23]

Galloway, in sum, left his readers with the inescapable conclusion that the Revolution might have been prevented and that the rebellion—once it was permitted to flare into hostilities—might have been crushed. Despite antecedents which made Anglo-American adversity unavoidable, the revolution ultimately resulted from costly British misapprehensions and evasions. The existence of some colonial malcontents could not, in the nature of things, have been avoided. But unsound colonial institutions favored the radicals, and unwise British decisions after 1765 terminated in the spectacular increase of American rebels. Nevertheless, Galloway still believed that the insurgents never comprised more than a small minority of the colonists, and in the end they triumphed largely through an amalgam of luck, terrorism, and the assistance rendered by traitors both within and outside the British government.

Considering the conditions under which Galloway wrote his history of the Revolution, the product was a remarkably sophisticated assessment. The study was meant to serve the dual functions of history and political disputation. It was produced hurriedly by a man of affairs who happened to be an exiled loyalist. The work compared favorably with histories of the colonies' written by other loyalists. George Chalmers' ambitious study, for instance, did not examine the period after 1696. Studies by Jonathan Boucher and Alexander Hewit, both Anglican clergymen, somewhat resembled Galloway's study; but Boucher's inquiry was written nearly twenty years after Galloway published his history, and Hewit investigated the rebellion only in South Carolina and Georgia. Accounts compiled by other loyalists—for example, Thomas Hutchinson, Thomas Jones, a former supreme court justice from New York, and Peter Oliver, the last chief justice of colonial Massachusetts—were not published during their lifetimes and generally probed events only within the provinces in which they dwelled.

Galloway's historical works were not without bias, error, and omission. In the typically eighteenth-century manner he was too preoccupied with the existence of conspiracies. As an astute politician Galloway fully realized the prevalence of intrigue, but he exaggerated the connection between English and American radicals. He unfairly impugned the motives of British military officials. He erred severely in overestimating the number of colonial loyalists. His study also failed to appreciate the growth of nationalism—a phenomenon he could not fully comprehend and appreciate. Furthermore, in his overweening bitterness he misunderstood the position adopted by Pennsylvania's proprietary rulers, and he somewhat magnified the effect of Franklin's and Dickinson's roles during the crises. Nor was his appraisal of British conduct the same as it had been before the beginning of the war. Finally, he not unnaturally enhanced the importance of his compromise scheme of 1774.

But when compared to the conclusions reached through several generations of professional historical scholarship, Galloway's appraisal of the revolutionary period appears to have been essentially sound. He recognized that the rebellion sprang from a multiplicity of causes. He, like many subsequent scholars, emphasized the deleterious impact of religious dissenters and the effect of America's primitive condition on British institutions. He showed a tentative understanding of the role ideas played as causal factors. He was fully cognizant of 1763 as a pivotal year. Galloway clearly realized that both sides bore some responsibility for imperial troubles; few contemporary Whig histories, in fact, placed more blame on Great Britain than did Galloway. His criticism of the ministry's taxation and appeasement policies has been amply upheld by later scholarship. The economic determinism with which he explained the behavior of some colonial merchants, planters, and artisans has been recurrently echoed during this century. He stressed that the contest was essentially a constitutional struggle, a conclusion resoundingly endorsed by probably a majority of the so-called Neo-Whig scholars in recent years. Finally, if Galloway overemphasized the importance of English radicals, he was at least aware that they existed and exerted some influence on the colonists, facts which have been largely ignored by historians until quite recently.

Whatever its weaknesses and merits, the *Historical and Political Reflections* reinforces the impression that Galloway's ideology provides the key to an understanding of his loyalist behavior. Two essential themes leap out of his study. He insisted that a malaise deep within the fabric of American life jeopardized the empire. Unless corrected—preferably by the Plan of Union he had first unveiled in 1774—further rebellion would occur until the imperial union was at last severed. In addition, while he believed the illness had many causes, he maintained that the primary disorder was constitutional in nature and was repairable. His recognition, reiterated in his histories, that both sides had embraced false doctrines and were committed to abnormal policies helps to explain his seeming indecisiveness during the Anglo-American quarrel. It was neither timidity nor a fundamental irresolution that so often rendered Galloway inactive before 1774 or that caused him to lapse into indolence after the war began; it was the realization that events compelled him to make a Hobson's choice. In fact, only someone capable of perceiving that both sides had blundered and that both shared responsibility for the crisis could advocate a plan of compromise. His histories demonstrate that he was ideologically inclined toward compromise and that his actions were not merely the shabby ploys of a desperate politician. Events in 1776 finally forced him to make that Hobson's choice. Once again, however, his histories reveal his disposition. The ultraimperialist *Weltanschauung* he exhibited in his histories was nothing other than the philosophy he had developed as a provincial politician. Galloway's message as a historian, therefore, was similar to that manifested by Galloway the politician. When compelled to act, his strategy, unavoidably, was to strive for reform, to surgically remove the diseased organs. Tender a plan for constitutional reform, he urged, a scheme that required compromise of both parties. But seek the reform under the protective cloak of the empire. Galloway apparently reached these conclusions at some point in the 1760s. It was this ideology which impelled his behavior in the 1770s, and it was this point of view which characterized the histories he wrote in the 1780s.

6

Loyalists and the Union:
"The subordinate right and the one superior fountain"

There is a final mirror in which the mind of Joseph Galloway can be reflected. Usually, his conduct has been compared to that of his adversaries who won the revolutionary argument. The most recent study of Galloway, for example, compared his behavior with that of his partner Franklin; the vanquished seldom compare favorably to the victor. It might be instructive, therefore, to collate Galloway's ideology and behavior with those of other articulate loyalists.[1]

This chapter seeks to reveal the general loyalist ideology and to view Galloway from that context. Examined in this light, Galloway appears to have shared the conclusions of most important loyalists. But he differed from his compatriots in two salient respects. He carried his concepts to their natural conclusions, even though he recognized that such action was certain to leave him exposed and vulnerable, and he overcame the pitfall of indecisiveness. He did act to prevent the rebellion, a task which few major loyalists undertook while there was still time to extinguish the holocaust.

Those who opposed the Revolution were a diverse assemblage. Many resisted the popular movement as early as 1765; in fact, some were virtually driven from their homeland by hostile mobs at that time. Others decided to oppose the American leadership only at a much later date. Loyalist leaders came from throughout the colonies and from a multiplicity of backgrounds. It would be foolhardy to maintain that a single loyalist ideology existed. Some loyalists, from a deep, innate conservatism, rushed to defend every British action. Many carried lifelong ideological commitments to their logical conclusions and embraced Britain as the only legitimate sovereign government and as the only polity which could adequately defend the impotent colonies. The ideology of others confronted them with the terrible choice of humbly conceding submission or acknowledging the rebellion.

It would be equally absurd to suggest that all loyalists acted from ideological conviction. It is difficult to determine what motivated the loyalists because, as Mary Beth Norton observed, "loyalism can be defined only in a negative sense, only through its relationship to the movement it opposed. . . . This is why loyalists were such a diverse group, and why it is practically impossible to delineate any characteristic common to them all, except their adherence to Great Britain." Wallace Brown, another student of loyalist behavior, noted nine distinct possibilities among the "welter of loyalist motives." His list ranged from economic opportunism to psychological necessity to the tug of religious and political ideology.[2]

Even if it is inaccurate to say that a single loyalist ideology existed, the conclusion is warranted that most articulate anti-revolutionaries shared a reasonably common ideology. No scholar would maintain, for instance, that a single radical outlook existed, but most would probably agree that the concepts in the Declaration of Independence generally reflected the mainstream of revolutionary philosophy. Similarly, while the opponents of the Revolution expressed diverse and often conflicting principles, a core of doctrine existed in their literature with which most would have felt comfortable. Moreover, although it might be acknowledged that the loyalists acted from diverse motives, it might also be recognized that ideology aroused those who opposed the revolution to the same extent that it provoked the rebellion's most fervent supporters.

Like Galloway, most loyalist writers appraised political questions from the perspective—and through the interests and biases—of the privileged upper class. Many were alarmed at the drift of dissenting ideology and feared that as a result of republican rhetoric the "people have been taught a dangerous truth, that all power is derived from them." No concept could have been more objectionable to most loyalist writers. Governments, they believed, must be constructed in such a fashion that no interest group could become omnipotent. It was especially important that the government not be seized by the masses, for such an occurrence would produce democratic anarchy, followed inevitably by the arbitrary repression of a dictatorship. Most of the leading loyalists observed the masses—the "lower sort," or the "meaner sort," as they were commonly called—with a jaundiced eye. Jonathan Boucher, an Anglican clergyman from Maryland, thought the common folk "particularly unworthy and unamiable." He believed the masses were "wrongheaded, ignorant, and prone to resist authority." Other loyalists referred to commoners as the "giddy, ignorant people," the "admiring vulgar," the graduates of the "Log College." Boucher thought egalitarian concepts were absurd. Not only were men not born with equal assets, he argued, but life naturally tended to magnify the differences between men. Those born to a higher station found that the "genteel life" made one "not quite so awkward and uncouth." Boucher's fellow clergyman Charles Inglis, a New York Anglican, agreed and contended that it was the "Duty of all Men" to be content with the station fate had provided for them. Unfortunately for the loyalists, a Georgia lady observed, in times of revolution "everywhere the scum rose to the top."[3]

In spite of the special fear of the "meaner sort," most loyalists believed that all men acted "not according to right, but according to present interest, and most according to passion." Boucher genuinely reflected loyalist sentiments when he wrote that the "predominant Passions in the Breasts of most Men" were "Ambition and Lust of Power above the Laws." The loyalists therefore devoted considerable attention to the problem of restraining those turbulent, primitive passions which motivated men. Unless checked, the passions natural to mankind constituted a formidable threat to liberty. Some rigidly defined liberty as the privilege of doing what is proper in the eyes of God. Others thought "perfect Freedom" could not be attained "until the Constitution of human Nature is changed," but added that "civil liberty" could exist if man surrendered some rights, such as the right of revenge or the right to use his own opinion to determine right from wrong. All agreed that liberty was a precious commodity which could easily be lost. One theorist told his readers that the "surest Way to lose Liberty is to abuse it." Most felt liberty was betrayed when "all are Masters" and none are the governed.[4]

To preserve liberty, some attempted to make a virtue of obedience. Boucher argued that anarchy could better be prevented through a careful molding of the "Manners and Morals of the People" than through the search for a perfect constitutional framework. Others maintained that dissent against lawful authority was contrary to the will of God and contended that defiance of the law was "inconsistent with [a] profession of *christianity*." Resistance to rulers authorized by God, one congregation was told, would produce the "wildest uproar and most unusual confusion." Cadwallader Colden, the lieutenant governor of New York, argued that rigorous indoctrination as to the place one occupied in society would thwart leveling tendencies. He regarded Anglican clergymen as the best qualified propagandists and recommended that a seminary be founded in America to produce scores of men of this persuasion.[5]

Most loyalists disagreed, however, and argued that the masses could

THE LOYALIST MIND

be adequately controlled only by government. "It has been proved," a loyalist argued, "that liberty can have no existence without obedience to the laws." The purpose of government was "to place man . . . out of the reach of his own power" in order to protect society. Without law as a restraint the "strongest would be master, the weakest [would] go to the wall; right, justice and property must give way to power."[6]

Without government the happiness and progress of mankind was impossible. Samuel Seabury, a New York Anglican, summarized his faction's concept of society when he argued that

> Government was intended *for* the security of those who live under it;—to protect the weak against the strong; the good against the bad;—to preserve order and decency among men, preventing everyone from injuring his neighbor.[7]

Like Galloway, most loyalists readily agreed that the best government was one in which the several interests in society were balanced one against another. The greatest dangers to stability and freedom arose when power was concentrated in the hands of one person or class or when absolute liberty was tendered to the people. If the democratic interests—the masses—were permitted uncontrolled sway, society would soon experience chaos; if the aristocratic interests alone ruled, mankind would soon feel the tyranny of an oligarchy. To prevent these "numberless inconveniences," an "equal poize" between branches was sought. Each branch was to constitute a restraint on the others so there would be "no means to admit of [their] doing wrong."[8]

The loyalists, including Galloway, regarded republicanism as the greatest threat to the established order; they used the terms "republican" and "democratic" synonymously and with equal reproach. Republican government, they believed, would inordinately shift the balance of power to the masses. Such a state of affairs, Thomas Hutchinson maintained, would mean the surrender of government to "the rabble," to those unfit to govern. The loyalist attorney general of Virginia, John Randolph, thought the " 'ignorant vulgar are as unfit to judge of the modes, as they are unable to manage the reins, of government.' " Most loyalists were certain that republicanism would produce a variety of evils. Frequent elections, one writer complained, afford "an opportunity for insatiable ambition, lawless faction, and horrid conspiracy to rear their monstrous heads." Unscrupulous politicians, a Maryland loyalist said, will flatter the voters in order to enact "their criminal designs." These unsavory types were the more unscrupulous because they realized that republicanism "never did, nor ever will answer in politics." Many Tories believed both civil war and foreign war to be inevitable companions of republicanism. Other Tories argued that the very concept of republicanism implied the destruction of authority and that this form of government would propel a society " 'next door to anarchy.' "⁹

Loyalists divided over the concept of popular government. Although some deplored the practice, Galloway and most loyalists agreed that the election of one branch of government was desirable. But most loyalists thought the electorate's control of the representatives ceased following the election. Hutchinson thought it absurd for elected representatives to seek instructions from the citizenry. Town meetings were nothing more than "mob meetings," he complained. Peter Oliver, chief justice of the Massachusetts Supreme Court, thought it a strange concept which decreed that a man was not free unless he consented to his rulers. Were men who were too ill to vote on election day denied liberty? Or, were those who voted for a losing candidate unfree? Was mankind enslaved if the legislature was malapportioned? Oliver's answer, like Hutchinson's, was to concede the voters a check on their representation only at election time.¹⁰

As with Galloway, this view of the inherent depravity of men and of the absolute necessity to structure government according to the three traditional social estates influenced the manner in which many moderates viewed events after 1765. Moreover, the logic of this ideology formed the eventual underpinning of loyalist imperial concepts and caused many colonists to choose to remain under the protective cloak of Great Britain following the beginning of hostilities.

A pivotal point of loyalist theory was the contention that the colonists were British citizens who had never left Britain's jurisdiction. From the earliest exploration of America the colonies had been just another part of the realm. When a nation acquired territory, they contended, the new domain simply became a part of the state. Consequently, Englishmen transplanted to the colonies had never left the nation, never entered the state of nature. The colonists continued both to possess all rights of Englishmen and to owe full allegiance to the English government.

It was essential to the loyalist argument to prove that the entire English government had participated in the founding of the colonies. Such an argument was made necessary by the radical contention that the only legitimate link between the colonies and the mother country was the crown. The rebels maintained that the new lands had been discovered by explorers acting under commissions issued only by the crown, and that the crown alone had issued the charters of incorporation. Furthermore, some revolutionaries argued that England had merely acquired, not annexed, America and held the region through the doctrine of feudal tenure. Many loyalists regarded the attacks on Parliament by American whigs as too preposterous to need a response. Some, however, answered that past acquiescence in parliamentary legislation demonstrated that the colonists traditionally had believed that the legislative branch shared in the founding of the colonies. Boucher assumed that the charters had been issued by a "parliamentary King" and that Americans were "Englishmen in the fullest Sense of the Word." Most, like Hutchinson, argued that either the charters had compelled obedience to Parliament or that "it was the sense of the Kingdom, that [Americans] were to remain subject to the supreme authority of Parliament." William Smith, Jr., a member of the Council in New York, maintained that because Parliament had been "conversant of the Grants and Charters of their Kings and Queens" the colonies were "not merely royal and crown created, but National and parliamentary Establishments."[11]

The fulcrum of loyalist logic was the assumption that the charters clearly placed each colony in a position of inferiority with regard to the English government. "Massachusettensis" and "Novanglus," Daniel Leonard and John Adams, debated the issue at length in the spring of 1775. Leonard, a Massachusetts attorney and loyalist, maintained that the first American charters gave the colonial governments no authority other than simple police powers. The Massachusetts charter, he said, was so explicit that there could be no question of the colony's obligation to obey acts of Parliament. Adams countered with the argument that the earliest immigrants had agreed to a charter which was binding only on the first generation of colonists. Subsequent generations had adhered to the covenant voluntarily and could withdraw their consent at any time; as a result of the language of the charters, and because America had never been formally annexed to Britain, the colonists owed allegiance only to the British crown. Adams asserted that Parliament had no power through natural law, common law, or statutory law to exercise authority over the colonists. He denied that the colonists had ever recognized the power of Parliament to do more than regulate the trade of the empire, and even this power existed "not by any principle of common law, but merely by the consent of the colonists."[12]

Thomas Chandler, a friend of Galloway, and Martin Howard of Rhode Island analyzed the charters and concluded that parliamentary authority over the colonies was as unlimited as over all other parts of the empire. Howard, a leader of the prerevolutionary Newport oligarchy, argued that the colonists had no rights independent of the charters. Each charter, he thought, guaranteed the individual rights of life, liberty, and property upon the colonists, and bestowed police power over internal affairs on the colonial government. William Smith regarded each charter as a "great National Covenant" which neither contracting party could unilaterally dissolve. Charters, he said, were imperial contracts under which the colonists agreed to become a small part of a great empire. This was not a traditional covenant between rulers and ruled, according to Smith, but a contractual relationship in which the Americans were compelled to weigh their rights in relation to the welfare of the empire as a whole. The "National Covenant," Smith wrote, bound England "to protect and promote the Colonies" and "obliged the Plantations to submit to her Authority" in all instances "not repugnant to their Grants . . . and established Privileges."[13]

Most loyalists, like Galloway, believed the colonists had subscribed to British sovereignty when they agreed to the charters. Jonathan Sewall, the royal attorney general in Massachusetts from 1767 to 1775, contended that the charters had not merely hinted at parliamentary sovereignty, but had "strongly and clearly" insisted upon such a condition. Chandler thought it absurd to believe that Parliament could have even considered founding colonies which could not be controlled by the supreme authority of the nation. "Can you imagine," he queried, "that in any instance, more than a *subordinate* right of jurisdiction was meant" by a charter?[14]

An equally crucial part of the loyalist ideology was the concept that every political entity must contain a sovereign authority. The idea of two sovereign authorities in the same state was, they insisted, an impossible contradiction. Seabury counseled that the "words *independence* and *colony* convey contradictory ideas: much like *killing* and *sparing*." When a "colony becomes independent [of] its parent state it ceases to be any longer a colony; just as when you *kill* a sheep, you cease to *spare* him." Hutchinson advised that he knew of no distinction which could be made between parliamentary sovereignty and colonial independence. A nation-state simply could not have two legislatures, for two assemblies would inevitably create two governments as distinct as England and Scotland before the Act of Union. If both the colonial assemblies and Parliament claimed to be sovereign, he thought "perpetual contention" would unavoidably arise and the state soon would be dismembered. One loyalist sought to defend the concept through the organic theory. As in the physical body, Isaac Hunt suggested, where life depended upon the operation of the heart, so in the body politic all subordinate jurisdictions flowed from "*one superior fountain.* Two distinct *independent powers* in one civil state are as inconsistent as two hearts in the same natural body," he added.[15]

Most loyalists argued that the power to tax must inevitably rest with the sovereign government. If denied the power of appropriation, a government could not be supreme. No government could endure without the power to raise its necessary funds. If Parliament was powerless to tax the colonies, it would soon have no colonies. Government consisted not only in the power to make and enforce legislation, but in the power of protection. So long as the colonies were under the British government and shared in its protection, the British government had a right to raise revenue.[16]

Although most loyalists agreed that Parliament was the sovereign legislative body for the empire, no unanimity existed over questions concerning that body's right to make policy for the colonists. In fact, the loyalists could not agree whether the colonists were even represented in Parliament. Many loyalists regarded it as an immutable law of nature that Americans could not be members of Parliament. Governor Hutchinson, for instance, believed the right of citizens to elect representatives was an ancient British prerogative, but he thought it impossible that the the rights of Englishmen could be the same in all parts of the dominion. While colonists should elect local representatives, he suggested, it was impractical to chose representatives for Parliament. The elected deputies could not adequately represent their constituents because of the immense distance between England and the colonies. Furthermore, American envoys would be so heavily outnumbered by English representatives that the practice of choosing members of Parliament would be of little benefit to the colonists. It was illogical to Hutchinson to assume that because a citizen had moved to distant provinces the central imperial government ceased to exercise authority over him. "Will it not rather be said that by this, their voluntary removal, they may have relinquished for a time at least, one of the rights of an English subject, which they might, if they pleased, have continued to enjoy, and may enjoy again, whensoever they will return to the place where it can be exercised?" Many Tories thought that colonists who contended their rights as Englishmen were violated were silly. Americans, they charged, never had the right to consent to the laws under which they lived. Many agreed with William Knox, a British subminister and agent for Georgia. "The *glorious rights, privileges* and *immunities*," he wrote, "which the *first settlers* in Virginia *carried with them*, appear to have been the *rights of being* governed by laws, enacted . . . in England. . . . It was their right and privilege . . . to be taxed by the King's *sole prerogative*, for the *use* and *benefit* of the Crown only, and in no case to be taxed by themselves, or their representatives elected by themselves." The colonists, he asserted, had agreed to submit to these arbitrary taxes in their charters.[17]

Others maintained that the colonists were, in fact, represented in Parliament through the concept of "virtual representation." Martin Howard thought consent "in substance and effect . . . was and ever will be, impracticable" for the colonists, but he did not deny that the Americans were represented in Parliament. The "right" to choose representatives was, in actuality, never the prerogative of all British citizens. "Let me ask," Howard queried, whether "the isle of Man, Jersey, or Guernsey [is] represented? What is the value or amount of each man's representation in the Kingdom of Scotland, which contains near two millions of people, and yet not more than three thousand have votes in the election of members of parliament?" Some people, in spite of their wealth, did not possess the franchise, he continued. In England "a worthless freeholder of forty shillings per annum can vote for a member of parliament, whereas a merchant, tho' worth a hundred thousand pounds sterling, if it consist only in personal effects, has no vote at all." Hence, the colonists could not claim for themselves a "right" of Englishmen which, in fact, never existed for Englishmen. The colonists had agreed in their charters to submit to the rule of Parliament, he asserted, and to adhere to Parliament was not to accept a violation of the rights of Englishmen, for colonials were represented "virtually" in the imperial legislature. The members of Parliament "are the representatives of every British subject, wheresoever he be," and the interests of the colonies are as adequately managed by these legislators as if each had been directly elected by Americans. "The freedom and happiness of every *British* subject depends, not upon his share in elections, but upon the sense and virtue of the *British* parliament, and these depend reciprocally upon the sense and virtue of the whole nation," he concluded.[18]

Many who opposed the rebellion, however, rejected the notion of "virtual representation" and, like their adversaries, regarded subjugation to an unrepresentative body as tyranny. Daniel Dulany, a member of the Maryland Council who ultimately remained a neutralist during the war, scored the most telling blow against "virtual representation." In a widely circulated pamphlet issued as an attack on the Stamp Act, Dulany contended that "the expression virtual representation [was] a fanciful phrase . . . a mere cob-web, spread to catch the unwary, and intangle the weak." Englishmen who did not possess the franchise might someday acquire the right to vote; they might even be elected to sit in Parliament. But Americans could look forward to neither prospect, for regardless of the amount of wealth a colonist accumulated, he could never expect to vote for a member of the Commons or sit in either house of Parliament. He even admitted that the nonvoting Englishman was "virtually" represented. Parliament could not pass tyrannical legislation against the disfranchised without "their oppression [falling] also upon the electors and representatives. The one can't be injured and the other indemnified." But the interests of colonists and inhabitants of the mother country were not always similar. Englishmen in the legislature could tax colonials without being adversely affected by the tax. In fact, legislation which was "oppressive and injurious to the colonies . . . might become popular in England, from the promise or expectation, that the very measures which depressed the colonies, would give ease to the Inhabitants of Great Britain."[19]

Dulany, however, did not persevere. He had no intention, Bernard Bailyn notes, of following "the implications of his own arguments." His action strikes at the heart of the ideological problem which confronted the loyalists. To reject the concept of "virtual representation" was to face the

THE LOYALIST MIND

alternatives of admitting that Parliament could make "all laws whatsoever" for the colonies or of acknowledging the radical claim that the colonists were not subject to a legislature in which they were unrepresented. The loyalists were in unanimous agreement that every government could have but one sovereign and that for the empire the British government—King, Lords, and Commons—constituted the sovereign entity. Moreover, loyalists were in general agreement on the imperial powers of the monarchy. But they were deeply divided on the proper limits of the power of Parliament over the colonies.[20]

The common link between the varied loyalist points of view was the concept of imperial nationalism—the notion that the empire must somehow be preserved. Fearful of making the "leap into the dark" which separation from England entailed, most loyalists fervently embraced and defended the concept of imperial union. One line of reasoning was to exalt the virtues of the imperial government. Daniel Leonard found it difficult to conceive of provincial governments under less control by the supreme polity. Virtually every loyalist agreed that Britain possessed the "most perfect system" of government that "the wisdom of the ages has produced."[21]

A pervasive aspect of pro-British thought was the belief that America required the protection of England. Some described the relationship between the mother country and colonies as akin to that of parents and children; others thought of the colonial relationship as synonymous with marriage, so that one partner should be dominant, and each should be "ready to acknowledge the merits, to pardon the faults, and condescend the weakness" of the other. All agreed that should America attain independence the idyllic Anglo-American relationship would be supplanted by an American democracy. Once outside the empire, the delicate balance between excess liberty and absolute tyranny would collapse.[22]

Other loyalists attempted to prove that a terrible civil war inevitably would follow any attempt at independence. One saw the colonists at a fork in the road with one branch leading to public tranquillity while the other led to anarchy and civil insurrection. Many regarded civil warfare as the worst of all evils. Such cataclysmic events usually resulted in the despotism of demagogues who drew power from the "violent temper and ungoverned passions" of the multitude.[23]

In addition to the evils unleashed by a civil war, the loyalists maintained that a war with England would bring disaster for America. Most loyalists thought it improbable that the colonies could win such a war. The colonies were disunited and lacking in trained troops. Americans were peaceful farmers and, as such, would be no match for professional British troops. The colonists were "without fortresses, without discipline, without military stores, without money." Whereas the colonists were ill-equipped for soldiering, Daniel Leonard maintained that the British soldiers had been "bred to arms" since infancy and had "already reaped immortal honors in the iron harvest of the field." The Americans were told that in the event of war they should anticipate no foreign assistance. All foreign trade would be eliminated by an English naval blockade; the Dutch were too involved in commercial intercourse with England to assist the colonies, while France had not forgotten "the drubbing" she sustained in the recent war. Nor was divine intervention to be anticipated. "God," a Tory wrote, "is a God of order and . . . he commands you to submit to your rulers . . . and therefore can never be supposed to favor *traitors* and *rebels*."[24]

If the colonists somehow defeated England, America's diplomatic problems would hardly cease. The greatest danger would be that a victorious, but prostrate, America would be easy prey for greedy European powers. Boucher imagined a scene in which "Goths and Vandels" overran the colonists. Leonard thought it was not a question of whether an independent America would be crushed, but only a matter of which power would be the first to seize North America. Although exhausted by a long war, America would have to contend with France and Spain, who were depicted as lusting after their former New World territories. The traditional American fear of encirclement was revived. Bound by the French and Spanish to the north, west, and south, and by Britain on the east coast, the colonists would face a combination of powers sufficient to "check our prosperity, or reduce us to the most abject state of slavery."[25]

Most loyalists were equally worried about the economic consequences of separation from Britain. Sever the imperial ties, a British official warned, and "there is an end to your trade, and a total loss of your property." Some loyalists mentioned the advantage of trading under the protective cloak of the British fleet, others stressed the desirability of English manufactured items. The empire alone freed America from the "wooden shoes of France, or the uncombed hair of Poland." In sum, a New Yorker observed, maintenance of the empire was of more than just "Importance . . . [or] even of vast Importance."[26]

Some loyalists held forth a vision of a glorious imperial future. In the empire the colonists were guaranteed both economic and military benefits by England without being relegated to a second-class citizenship. Americans had an uncommonly free judicial system as well as considerable religious independence. One essayist, moreover, alleged that Britain's encouragement of colonial industry had converted America from a "desert and howling wilderness . . . into a flourishing and populous country." William Smith believed that even if colonial rights were occasionally trampled Americans were compelled to recognize that their domain formed but a part of a great empire. He implored his fellow colonists to overcome provincialism and think in

THE LOYALIST MIND

imperial terms. To Smith the "antient Union" meant "Ties of Justice, Humanity, Patriotism, Benevolence, Honor, Religion and Interest." Jonathan Sewall asked the colonists to compare their status with that of other peoples. "The truth is," he asserted, "we have been lifted up to heaven in privileges, and now like the chosen people of old, we spurn the hand that raised and has hitherto sustained us."[27] According to Massachusettensis,

> Our merchants are opulent and our yeomenry in easier circumstances than the noblese of some states. . . . Schools, colleges, and even universities are interspersed through the continent: Our country abounds with foreign refinements, and flows with exotic luxuries. These are the infallible marks not only of opulence but of freedom.[28]

Hence the loyalist quandary. Although all loyalists were convinced that the empire must somehow be preserved, deep divisions existed over the colonists' proper place within the empire as well as over the best manner through which to maintain the Anglo-American union. The loyalists were able to reach the nearly unanimous agreement that the only means of seeking reconciliation was through a petition to the crown. Loyalists variously described the means to reconciliation as "respectful representations," a blend of "decent acquiescence with . . . tolerable requistions," a "dutiful and rational remonstrance." Some merely urged the colonists to "act in a constitutional way, by proper addresses," or to "employ those methods of redress, which the constitution admits." The loyalists, however, divided over whether a national congress or the colonial assemblies should issue the petition; Chandler, Boucher, and Seabury believed a congress would be satisfactory if the gathering was broadly representative and sanctioned by the crown.[29]

The loyalists were also deeply divided over the best manner of imperial union. A few Tories believed the fate of the empire should hinge upon granting seats in Parliament to the colonists. Governor William Franklin thought this the most appealing solution to Anglo-American differences, but he added that the reform should also be extended to all English citizens and the inhabitants of Ireland. Some loyalists merely advocated a return to the pre-1763 imperial condition. Others proposed acceptance of the English peace offer of 1775—a plan which acknowledged a Parliament in which America was unrepresented as the sovereign legislative body for the union. After the war commenced many urged that the colonists accept Lord North's peace proposal of 1778 as a basis for reconciliation; this scheme would have given the colonists nearly everything which Congress had demanded in 1774. The most widely offered suggestion was that a compromise solution be reached by which the sovereignty of Parliament would be recognized by the colonists but at the same time the Americans would be protected constitutionally against arbitrary taxation. Charles Inglis thought a compromise under which Parliament would neither tax America nor be compelled to formally relinquish its right to tax the colonists offered the best prospects for peace. Seabury hoped a formal imperial constitution would be written which would designate the limits of British sovereignty while it secured the rights and property of the colonists.[30]

Aside from Galloway's scheme, the most elaborate plan for reconciliation was devised by William Smith, Jr., of New York. Scion of a powerful political family, Smith followed in his father's footsteps. Following his graduation from Yale, he practiced law and joined the Presbyterian faction in New York politics. In 1752 he became an editor of *The Independent Reflector*, one of America's earliest magazines and a journal that mirrored England's radical publications. Smith's scheme was devised sometime between 1765 and 1767; although it was never formally presented, he did suggest portions of the plan to influential English officials. He believed reconciliation was essential because the imperial impasse was akin to a "disease that affects Life." The remedy for the imperial malady was a new constitution to govern relations between England and the colonies. Smith argued that the old constitution was created before the founding of the colonies and was designed only as a framework for the government of England. Constitutions, he thought, "ought to bend and *sooner* or *later* will bend." Since a "*new, adventitious State* had developed in the intervening years, it was insensible" to use this constitution for an imperial structure. He thought it unwise for the existing Parliament to legislate for the colonies. Even if the colonists were seated in Parliament, he said, the empire would become "too complex, popular and unwieldy" for one body to act as the sole legislative power. The majority in Parliament, furthermore, would always be "utterly incompetent" to pass on American affairs. Therefore, Smith proposed the creation of a "Parliament of North America" consisting of a "Lord Lieutenant," a Council with at least twenty-four of its members appointed by the crown, and a House of Commons composed of deputies elected by each colonial assembly. The crown would designate the amount of revenue America must contribute for the maintenance of the empire, and the North American parliament would, in turn, determine each colony's assessment. Each colonial assembly would decide how it would gather its quota. His plan would have retained the veto power of the crown, as well as Parliament's "Legislative Supremacy, in *all Cases* relative to *Life Liberty* and *Property*, except in the Matter of *Taxations* for *general Aids*, or its immediate, internal support of the American Government." Smith recognized that England might not agree to a "*third Parliament*" because of "a Jealousy"; but, he added, "this very Jealousy, is part of the National Disease, and will if it continues, be the Ruin of us all." Smith hoped the colonies would be at liberty to appoint agents to negotiate with London for reconciliation. "Overtures of this kind," he concluded, "will not only promote a firm Union among ourselves by satisfying scruples of many conscientious Persons but by demonstrating to the whole World the Purity of our Intentions."[31]

But, typically, Smith communicated his ideas neither to Galloway nor to other loyalists. Throughout the crisis the loyalists remained disorganized and often appeared muddled and confused. Their actions during much of the upheaval seemed timid. When the stamp duties were enacted, for instance, many colonists found the legislation distasteful but supported the parent state nonetheless. The behavior of Jared Ingersoll, a stamp tax collector in Connecticut, was not uncommon. Originally an opponent of the act, he later defended and attempted to enforce the measure. Governor Hutchinson deplored the act and informed British officials of his attitude. But publicly he said nothing, and he watched silently as his reputation was irredeemably damaged in Massachusetts and his potential influence on colonial moderates was severely diminished. On the other hand, some loyalists vigorously opposed the legislation. William Smith, Jr., reported his displeasure to high British officials and drafted the hostile New York Resolves of December 1765. William Samuel Johnson, later a Connecticut loyalist, wrote his colony's anti-stamp tax resolves in October 1765. Both attacked the act as a violation of the right of colonists to be taxed only by their elected representatives. It was inconceivable, Johnson wrote, that officials elected in England could "dispose of our property." The "only legal Representatives of the Inhabitants of this Colony," he added, "are the Persons they elect to serve as Members of the General Assembly thereof." Smith lamented that this "single Stroke has lost Great Britain the Affection of all her Colonies." Daniel Dulany attacked the act with a devastating pamphlet; he was subsequently elected to represent Maryland in the Stamp Act Congress. Loyalist confusion and equivocation in 1765 might, however, be excused. As Norton notes, during the early crises "the political and ideological lines were not at all clearly drawn. . . . There could be no loyalists until there were rebels, and there were no rebels until after 1773." In 1765 the opposing factions quarreled "not so much over *whether* to protest . . . as over *how* to protest."[32]

Those who later opposed the revolution remained just as divided during the Townshend Duty crisis of 1767 to 1770. A few defended the legislation. Some like Dulany urgently attacked the taxes and even supported the colonial boycott of British products. More often than not, the eventual loyalists merely tried to restrain those in opposition to the act.[33]

The loyalists did not act with much concert until after the meeting of the Continental Congress late in 1774. The failure of that body to pursue compromise stung the moderates. An explosion of pamphlets resulted, some groping to defend the British, others agonizing over colonial actions and warning of the likely consequences of confrontation. Some essayists denounced Congress for its "high treason" and its virtual "open declaration of hostilities." But the loyalists had waited far too long. By 1775 they were overwhelmed by events.[34]

Viewed from this context of loyalist ideology, Galloway's attitudes and actions during the maelstrom of rebellion are more easily seen and assessed. His outlook is revealed as less that of an isolated dreamer or terribly antiquated theoretician, less a contemptible schemer, than that of an ideologist in the mainstream of a large, viable, pervasive school of early American thought. Galloway's appraisal of the baleful aspects of human nature and his remedy for these ills fell squarely amidst the principal avenues of loyalist logic. His anxieties about the masses, about republicanism, about the basic sources of human conduct, appear less extraordinary; his rallying to British institutions—to balanced government, for instance— seems more commonplace. Nor was his tendency to examine imperial affairs through the same theoretical eyes with which he scrutinized provincial occurrences in the least unusual. His views on sovereignty, on the powers of Parliament, and on the legitimate manner of American dissent were all underscored and embraced by other anti-revolutionary philosophers.

From this perspective Galloway's behavior appears less equivocal, evasive, and indecisive than some have alleged. Like most of his loyalist compatriots, he groped and searched for some meaning to the events which swirled about him. In the end his answer was not startling. The empire had to be saved, he concluded. Not only was America unprepared for independence, but the prospect of a brilliant, expansive Anglo-American partnership was too alluring to be permitted to vanish. In place of the empire, he thought, the radicals offered republicanism, fuzzy theorems concerning sovereignty, and the very real likelihood of persistent turmoil.

But Galloway differed from most other loyalists in a fundamental respect. He perceived more quickly the necessity to reconstitute the empire, and he pushed for that goal continually—from the earliest crises until after the Revolution was over. The manner of imperial reform which he advocated fell easily within the broad amalgam of loyalist thought, and, like Smith's somewhat similar scheme, crystallized the essence of loyalist consciousness. He concluded that both Great Britain and the American leadership were constitutionally correct. The empire must have but one sovereign legislative body as the British leaders insisted. However, the colonial leaders properly maintained that the rights of Americans were violated because they possessed no share in the weighty imperial decisions. Galloway realized that the conflicting parties would inevitably cause strife resulting in American submission or independence unless they agreed to a compromise settlement. Compromise demanded that each factious party acknowledge certain truths in the ideology of its opponent; compromise, furthermore, would necessitate the reconstruction of the Anglo-American union so as to make future upheaval unlikely. When Dulany and others reached this abyss in their reasoning, they feared to pursue the "implications of [their] own arguments." Galloway persevered. The only alternative to revolution or submission was compromise attended by imperial reform. By the late 1770s most loyalists and many British officials reached the conclusion arrived at much earlier by Galloway. But by then it was too late to save the empire.

7

Conclusion

By any reasonable standard of evaluation Joseph Galloway was a failure. Over a span of fifteen years he rose to the summit of power in colonial Pennsylvania, but within another decade his position had atrophied, and he was secluded at Trevose in retirement. Four years later he was trapped in exile in London. Each of his great aspirations remained unfulfilled. He had been unable to procure a compromise agreement which might have forestalled Anglo-American hostilities. Once the rebellion began he had not been able, despite a spate of pamphlets, to alter British military strategy. His struggle to preserve and reform the imperial relationship had been ineffectual. Although he fancied himself a theoretician, he had not left behind so much as a single memorable phrase. The doctrines he so prolifically championed, moreover, had born no fruit in either his native country or his adopted state.

Galloway's background provides clues to his eventual loyalist behavior, although before the imperial crisis his career was hardly distinguishable from that of dozens of other enterprising Americans who later played an active role during the rebellion. He was born to affluent parents, married into an even wealthier and more powerful family, established a flourishing legal practice, fraternized with his colony's most influential social and political figures. Well before his thirtieth birthday Galloway had attained a seat in the Pennsylvania Assembly and was an acknowledged associate of the venerated Franklin. His provincial policies were popular and seemed to accurately reflect the common wishes of his generation. His support of Great Britain during the French and Indian War reflected majority sentiment in the East as well as in the beleaguered West, and it proved to be so popular that it provided the means by which he successfully launched his political career. Nor is there any reason to discount the popularity of the anti-proprietary movement, at least before 1765; and his attempts to transform the system of judicial tenure in Pennsylvania elicited genuine approbation.

Like most Americans, Galloway did not manifest a well-developed, coherent ideological outlook before the imperial crisis. As a student of the law and an articulate and enlightened provincial, he expressed merely a jumble of ideas in his initial speeches and pamphlets. In these early writings he relied on the thoughts of a few English theorists and legalists as well as a handful of renowned continental authors with whom every educated colonist would have been thoroughly familiar.

Nevertheless, after 1765 Galloway reacted to events through this patina of ideology. These sentiments led him to recoil from radical rhetoric. He found much in the language of dissent which offended his sense of good government. The exhortations of the popular leaders, he suggested, implied an attachment to republicanism—a doctrine filled with irksome qualities. He detected a turning away from the traditional concepts of government, and he was apprehensive lest the colonists strain the delicate equilibrium between liberty and authority. He quickly perceived that the developing American notion of sovereignty, if carried to its logical conclusion, would shatter the imperial union. Unavoidably, the American position would lead to a denial of all Parliamentary powers. And, he acknowledged, if a sovereign imperial legislature did not exist, an empire could not exist.

Still, Galloway shared many sentiments with the popular leaders. He did not live in a vacuum. He and the radicals read the same newspapers and pamphlets, were nurtured in the same primitive New World environment, saw events through the eyes of colonists and as Britons. He, like the popular leaders, found the imperial arrangement wanting in many respects. But for Galloway the nature of the provincial governments constituted the most striking defect; improperly—perhaps even illegally—constructed, these polities fostered repugnant traits which tore at the fabric of colonial society. However, Galloway agreed with the contention of radicals that Great Britain violated the colonists' rights as Englishmen. He recognized a need for parliamentary legislation because of that body's sovereign nature and because of the financial exigencies of the union. But he also acknowledged the illegitimacy of a legislative body acting on behalf of the unrepresented colonists. Without a reformation, he sadly conceded, the colonies would be subjected to a tyrannical imperial power.

Galloway has frequently been depicted as pusillanimous and equivocal. He was neither. He understood the dangers inherent in both sides of the quarrel, and he sought a middle ground. To embrace the logic of the American leadership, he believed, was to flirt with colonial independence, to risk an American tyrant, to hazard social instability. If the rebellion succeeded, his fervent hope for a majestic, expanding, acquisitive American future would be demolished. Galloway and other imperial nationalists confidently looked forward to the day when a mighty collection of colonies would stand with Great Britain in an omnipotent Anglo-American union. In such an empire America would be sufficiently secure from foreign threats, and powerful enough, to exert its will throughout the New World. On the other hand, to exalt the obsequious position of the doctrinaire Tories, he admitted, was to invite British tyranny and oppression. Hence he believed that accommodation through compromise offered the only viable alternative to discord and despotism.

Galloway's first object in the early crises, however, was merely to prevent disorder, the malady he saw as the great immediate danger. Violence would efface the social bonds and decimate the ruling oligarchy within the province. Man, acting from his natural, selfish desire for gain, would seek to exploit the ferment; but ultimately he would crave security, a yearning which would lead him to embrace any form of government— regardless of its distasteful and imprudent qualities—which promised to ward off disorder. Therefore, although he urged reform and advocated the abandonment of those imperial features which made the British rule objectionable, he was concerned that the American appeal for redress be made in a legal, constitutional manner. He refused to join with those who engaged in economic boycotts and street riots. Only the petitions of elected American assemblies, whether national or provincial, were legitimate for seeking repeal of parliamentary legislation and pressing for reform.

It is not clear when Galloway concluded that the impasse could be peaceably settled only through compromise. He may have reached the conclusion as early as the Stamp Act crisis; certainly his statements at that time strongly suggest a willingness to compromise. He may not have grasped what was really occurring before 1770 when he was compelled to abandon his customary Assembly seat and seek reelection from a conservative rural area. At any rate, by 1774 he was fully aware of the revolutionary nature of the situation as well as of the obstreperous and defiant stance which both parties had assumed. That year, at last in a position of preeminence in the Continental Congress, he revealed the scheme which he believed would forestall Anglo-American hostilities. He did not seek compromise from timidity—a timid soul could hardly have espoused compromise in the highly charged atmosphere which prevailed in Philadelphia in 1774—but because his *Weltanschauung* led him to appreciate the logic of both parties. He desired the best of both worlds. The quintessence of his hope was that a strong, tranquil imperial union might be maintained which would not impinge on the liberties of the colonists. Provincial reform, he believed, offered the greatest hope for stability and order, and presented the best prospect for the maintenance of human rights. Loyalty to the parent state also provided the best hope for the protection of America's economic and defense priorities.

Galloway's compromise and reform plan would have acknowledged British hegemony, yet it would have extended a share of those powers to the subjects living in the American colonies. Both the imperial and provincial governments would have been reconstituted. The local governments would have been renovated and made into royal colonies—a reform, he confidently believed, which would have instituted at the parochial level a bulwark against those insidiously destructive and weakening tendencies which had plagued the old regimes and made the rebellion virtually unavoidable. In addition, the creation of an American branch of Parliament, he thought, would have revitalized the empire. Most rebels and loyalists fervently shared the belief that a balanced polity provided the best prospect for good government. Galloway's plan would have established a new balance within the Anglo-American union. Instead, however, of balancing only social estates Galloway, like Madison in *The Federalist*, would have balanced a variety of interest groups. Lords and Commons, he assumed, would continue to reflect the English point of view; the "third branch" would protect the outlook of America; and the King would be the union's impartial arbiter. Hence as the mixed government ideal provided safeguards against arbitrary class rule, Galloway's balanced union was to have protected colonial minorities against arbitrary imperial majorities.

No other loyalist offered such an extensive and bold solution to the imperial crisis. Many loyalists merely urged that the colonists petition the crown and rely on its good will. Some desired no alteration in the imperial structure and would have been satisfied to see the colonial dissenters silenced by British force. Aside from Galloway's scheme the most systematic loyalist plan to avert the rebellion by restructuring the empire was proposed by William Smith, Jr., of New York. His proposals, unlike those of Galloway, were never presented to a colonial legislative body, although they were secretly passed on to high imperial officials. Smith's proposals anticipated far less reconstruction than Galloway desired. Although Smith urged the creation of an American congress, he did not envision that legislature wielding autonomous powers in matters of imperial taxation. Imperial sovereignty under the Smith plan would have been lodged in a Parliament in which the colonists remained unrepresented; the purpose of the American congress was merely to implement policy decided upon in London. Furthermore, the Smith plan made no attempt to balance conflicting imperial interests, and, consequently, America was given no legal means to restrain British arbitrariness.

Galloway's behavior, however, was not unlike that of most loyalists. His ideology fell easily within the mainstream of loyalist principles. Like most loyalists, his apprehension of the common man, combined with his persistent disbelief that America was prepared to stand alone, compelled him to resist the colonial separatist movement. Furthermore, Galloway and most loyalists continued to support the traditional concept of imperial nationalism. The great difference between Galloway and most loyalists was that he acted resolutely throughout the crisis while most Tories vacillated or remained inactive until events overtook them and negated their contributions.

The Revolution demonstrated that many of Galloway's anxieties were groundless. America, of course, not only secured independence but avoided civil war and undue disturbance. Nor was the new nation seriously imperiled by foreign powers in the years following the war. Moreover, independent America's break with the past—with the ideology which Galloway and his colleagues proclaimed—was not as considerable as the loyalists had suspected it would be. Galloway must have watched from exile with amazement as his former adversaries constructed a national charter which resembled in many respects the imperial constitution he had advocated. A federal system emerged after 1787 in which the relationship of the states to the national polity was not unlike the status which Galloway recommended the colonies be permitted to assume toward the imperial government. The republican nature of the United States Constitution must have appalled Galloway, but he must have thought the new government consisted of prudently balanced branches. Although the three national wings of government differed decidedly from those Britain had established, one of the branches, the independent judiciary, embodied ideals Galloway had pursued a quarter century earlier. He must have been profoundly startled to witness state after state—Pennsylvania, among others, through a second constitution drafted in the immediate postwar period—establishing carefully balanced governments which approximated his concept of the ideal provincial entity. Even the principal rhetoric which accompanied the new government, the *Federalist* essays, bore striking similarities to Galloway's ideology. The essays abandoned the rhetoric of virtue which had accompanied the Revolution and depicted man's nature in a manner similar to Galloway's expostulations; rigid checks on man's liberties were justified, although with more republican eloquence, for the same reasons that Galloway had urged restraints on the "meaner sort." The *Federalist* defense of sovereignty bore a likeness to certain passages in the *Candid Examination*. Its lament of "faction," and Madison's famous scheme to mitigate the designs of "factious leaders," resembled Galloway's complaints concerning the colonists' dissembling pleas against the parent state and his antidote for the malady of divisiveness. There is no evidence that Galloway influenced the Federalists. The resemblance between the thought of the Founders and the loyalists merely reflected the fact that the ideology of the competing factions sprang from somewhat common sources and, despite insoluble differences, often drew upon like fears and aspirations.

Galloway's journey to exile, his failure, was partially of his own making. He consciously, rationally chose to remain loyal; he was privy to the same intellectual forces as the Whigs, and he might have chosen, as they did, to support the rebellion. Even as a loyalist he might have behaved differently and achieved more salutary results. He might have avoided unrewarding activities which weakened his political base in Pennsylvania and besmirched his reputation elsewhere. A more astute politician—Franklin, for instance—would have curtailed his anti-proprietary diligence after 1765 or 1766; the damaging Goddard affair need never have occurred, and perhaps the needless bickering with Dickinson and other luminaries might have been avoided. Had Galloway proposed a detailed compromise plan earlier than 1774 he might have found a more receptive audience. He and other moderates might have acted with more concert before the war. He might have refrained from shrill pamphleteering following the defeat of his plan by Congress. He might have attended the Second Continental Congress and continued to seek a nonviolent solution to the empire's woes. In light of the deep divisions within Pennsylvania—including, of course, the persistent anti-separatist feelings which lingered even after 1776—Galloway's continued presence in Congress ultimately might have proved a crucial obstacle to a unanimous declaration of independence. He might have acknowledged his loyalism at some earlier moment instead of waiting until the war was eighteen months old. Had he actively advised the British command throughout 1775 and 1776 the imperial strategy might have been altered, if only imperceptibly, and the failures which beset General Howe might have been avoided or lightened. Moreover, his demonstrative loyalism might have served as an example and activated like-minded colonists during those crucial early months of the war.

Despite his errors and omissions, Galloway's fate was probably sealed as soon as the earliest disturbances occurred. The activities of Galloway and of the radicals reflected the crystallization of the world view each had embraced in the safer, more tranquil prerebellion era. British reform policies acted as a catalyst which affected the sensibilities of scores of Americans. Conflict, rhetoric, anxiety, changed many people. Many colonists acquired a disrespect for British institutions and ideology. In the exigency of the times men confronted old notions, altered some concepts, scuttled others, and intuitively and defiantly clasped still other ideals. What few men realized in the drift and confusion of the moment was that a genuinely revolutionary situation was imminent, or perhaps that a revolution had already occurred—possibly as early as 1765. Once the imperial partners clashed over the Stamp Act, once the logic of each party was scrutinized, once the old ruling order had been challenged and had begun to crumble about the edges, perhaps there was no turning aside. Those who were transformed by occurrences after 1765 first exhibited an inclination to resist and ultimately the will to revolt.

Increasingly, however, Galloway's notions grew more archaic in the wake of events in the 1760s and 1770s. He and others of similar outlook reacted to the turbulence with a rigidity of spirit and inflexibility of manner. For this sect the old ways, the old institutions, the old ideas, increasingly assumed a hallowed meaning. The preservation of order became an end in itself. Galloway and his loyalist compatriots were able neither to understand the righteous impulse of the radical cause nor to comprehend the impact with which the transmogrification of the Anglo-American relationship had stunned their adversaries. Galloway was capable of understanding the altercation only in a constitutional manner, a viewpoint which made totally incomprehensible the moral indignation, the nationalistic fervor, the exuberant sense of mission manifested by the revolutionaries. In the tempestuous events which began with the Stamp Act men were guided in great measure by ideas. But whereas for the radicals the old ideology took on new meanings giving rise to meliorist longings, the old ideas enveloped Galloway in a fog which inhibited and deflected his response to the bewildering incidents that buffeted his world.

Notes

ESSAY ON THE SOURCES

The historian who studies Joseph Galloway is plagued by the scarcity of private papers. Most of Galloway's manuscript materials were destroyed during the Revolution. No large collections of his papers are extant, but some items are included with the Franklin papers at the American Philosophical Society, the Yale University Library, and the William L. Clements Library of the University of Michigan. Other items can be found in the Galloway papers at the Library of Congress, as well as the Gratz Collection, the Ferdinand J. Dreer Collection, and the Society Collection of the Historical Society of Pennsylvania. A few additional items may be found in the Thomson papers at the New York Public Library.

Some important private materials have been published. These include "Some Letters of Joseph Galloway," *Pennsylvania Magazine of History and Biography*, XXI (1897), 477–84; "The Diary of Grace Growden Galloway," Raymond C. Werner, ed., ibid., LV (1931), 32–96, and LVIII (1934), 152–92; and "Letters to Joseph Galloway, from Leading Tories in America," *The Historical Magazine*, VII (1912), 1–26, 150–65, 286–304, 337–56, VIII (1913), 34–50, 168–86, 235–56, 338–52, and IX (1914), 54–67, 232–41, 327–36.

Moreover, much about Galloway's role in the Pennsylvania Assembly can be extrapolated from the *Pennsylvania Archives*. The first four series of the *Archives* include the official papers and messages of the colony's governors; most applicable for Galloway, however, is *Pa. Archives*, 5th Ser. (Harrisburg: Harrisburg Publishing Co., 1906), and *Votes and Proceedings of the House of Representatives of the Province of Pennsylvania*, *Pa. Archives*, 8th Ser. (Harrisburg, 1931–35).

Galloway's activities at the national level may be seen in Volume I of *Journals of the Continental Congress, 1774–1879*, Worthington C. Ford, ed. (Washington: Government Printing Office, 1904–37). Also see *Letters of Members of the Continental Congress* (Washington: The Carnegie Institute, 1921–36), Edmund C. Burnett, ed.; Volume I of the *Letters* is especially useful, as is Volume II of *Diary and Autobiography of John Adams*, Lyman Butterfield, ed. (Cambridge: Harvard University Press, 1961). Some letters and an unpublished essay are printed in Volume X of the *Archives of the State of New Jersey, First Series*, William A. Whitehead, ed. (Newark: Daily Advertiser Printing Office, 1886). Important sources for Galloway as an international politician are Volumes XX through XXIII of *The Parliamentary History of England*, William Cobbett, ed. (London: T.C. Hansard, 1802–20), and Volumes IV and XXIV of *Facsimilies of Manuscripts in European Archives Relating to America, 1773–1783*, Benjamin Stevens, ed. (London: Malby and Sons, 1889–98).

Philadelphia was an important journalistic center during Galloway's lifetime, and Galloway was a prolific newspaper essayist. In addition to the *Pennsylvania Chronicle*, which he co-owned for a time, his essays—and those of other important politicians—appeared in the *Pennsylvania Gazette*, the *Pennsylvania Journal*, and the *Pennsylvania Packet*.

The most extensive sources of Galloway materials are his pamphlets and broadsides. Listed alphabetically these include: *A Candid Examination of the Mutual Claims of Great Britain, and the Colonies: with a Plan of Accommodation, on Constitutional Principles* (New York: James Rivington, 1775); *A Letter from Cicero to the Right Hon. Lord Viscount H—E: occasioned by his late speech in the House of C—ns* (London: J. Bow, 1781); *A Letter to the People of Pennsylvania, occasioned by the Assembly's passing that Important Act for Constituting the Judges* (Philadelphia, 1760); *A Letter to the Right Honorable Lord Viscount H—E* (London: J. Wilkie, 1779); *A Reply to an Address, to the Author of a Pamphlet, entitled, 'A Candid Examination of the Mutual Claims, etc.'* (New York: James Rivington, 1775); *A Reply to the Observations of Lieut. Gen. Sir William Howe, on a Pamphlet Entitled Letters to a Nobleman* (London: G. Wilkie, 1780); *A True and Impartial State of the Province of Pennsylvania* (Philadelphia: W. Dunlap,1759); *Advertisement, to the Public* (Philadelphia: B. Franklin and D. Hall, 1765); *An Account of the Conduct of the War in the Middle Colonies* (London: G. Wilkie, 1780); *An Address to the Freeholders and Inhabitants of the Province of Pennsylvania* (Philadelphia: Anthony Ambruster, 1764); *Cool Thoughts on the Consequences to Great Britain of American Independence. On the Expence of Great Britain in the Settlement and Defence of the American Colonies. On the Value and Importance of the American Colonies and the West Indies to the British Empire* (London: J. Wilkie, 1780); *Fabri-*

cus, or *Letters to the People of Great Britain on the Absurdity and Mischiefs of Defensive Operations only in the American War; and on the Causes of the Failure in the Southern Operations* (London: G. Wilkie, 1782); *Historical and Political Reflections on the Rise and Progress of the American Rebellion* (London: G. Wilkie, 1780); *Letters from Cicero to Cataline the Second* (London: J. Bow, 1781); *Letters to a Nobleman, on the Conduct of the War in the Middle Colonies* (London: J. Wilkie, 1779); *Observations on the Fifth Article of the Treaty with America: and on the Necessity of appointing a Judicial Enquiry into the Merits and Losses of the American Loyalists* (London: printed by order of the Agents, 1783); *Political Reflections on the Late Colonial Governments: in which their original Constitutional Defects are pointed out, and shown to have naturally produced the Rebellion, which has unfortunately terminated in the Dismemberment of the British Empire* (London: J. Wilkie, 1783); *Plain Truth: or, A Letter to the Author of Dispassionate Thoughts on the American War* (London: G. Wilkie and R. Faulder, 1780); *The Claim of the American Loyalists Reviewed and Maintained upon incontrovertible principles of law and justice* (London: G. and T. Wilkie, 1788); *The Examination of Joseph Galloway, Esq., Late Speaker of the House of Assembly of Pennsylvania, Before the House of Commons, in a Committee on the American Papers, with Explanatory Notes* (London: J. Wilkie, 1779); *The Speech of Joseph Galloway, Esq., in Answer to the Speech of John Dickinson, Esq.* (Philadelphia: W. Dunlap, 1764); *Tit for Tat, or the Score Wip'd Off* (New York, 1756); *To the Freeholders, and other Electors of Assemblymen for Pennsylvania* (Philadelphia: W. Dunlap, 1765).

A few important secondary studies of Galloway exist. The best and fullest treatment of Galloway before the rebellion is *Franklin and Galloway: A Political Partnership* (New Haven: Yale University Press, 1972), by Benjamin Newcomb. Also see David L. Jacobson's "John Dickinson and Joseph Galloway, 1764–1776: A Study in Contrasts" (Ph.D. dissertation, Princeton University, 1959). An incisive essay on Galloway's behavior as hostilities neared is Robert Calhoon's " 'I have Deduced Your Rights': Joseph Galloway's Concept of His Role, 1774–1775, "*Pennsylvania History*, XXXV (1968), 356–78. Several ground-breaking studies of Galloway and the Revolution exist. The best is Julian P. Boyd's *Anglo-American Union: Joseph Galloway's Plans to Preserve the British Empire, 1774–1788* (Philadelphia: University of Pennsylvania Press, 1941); Professor Boyd's study is essential not only for its analysis of Galloway, but because the study reprints all extant plans which Galloway devised after 1774. The reader must be aware, however, that a Plan of Union of 1785 which Boyd attributed to Galloway was, in fact, designed by Jonathan Sewall. Important information is also contained in Ernest H. Baldwin, "Joseph Galloway, the Loyalist Politician," *Pennsylvania Magazine of History and Biography*, XXVI

(1902), 161–91, 289–321, 417–42; Oliver Kuntzleman, *Joseph Galloway, Loyalist* (Philadelphia: Temple University Press, 1941); James H. Hutson, *Pennsylvania Politics 1740–1770: The Movement for Royal Control and Its Consequences* (Princeton: Princeton University Press, 1972); and Raymond C. Werner, "Joseph Galloway, his Life and Times" (Ph.D. dissertation, State University of Iowa, 1927).

Several important studies of the loyalists are available, and many of these comment on the activities of Galloway. Still useful is the early study by Claude H. Van Tyne, *Loyalists and the American Revolution* (New York: Burt Franklin Reprint, 1970). Important recent studies include William Nelson, *The American Tory* (Oxford: The Clarendon Press, 1961); Wallace Brown, *The Good Americans: The Loyalists in the American Revolution* (New York: William Morrow, 1969); and Robert M. Calhoon, *The Loyalists in Revolutionary America, 1765–1782* (New York: Harcourt Brace Jovanovich, 1972). For Pennsylvania Tories see *The Loyalists of Pennsylvania* (Columbus: Ohio State University Press, 1920), by Wilbur Sieburt. The most recent study of the loyalist refugees is Mary Beth Norton, *The British-Americans: The Loyalist Exiles in England, 1774–1789* (Boston: Little, Brown, 1972). For additional secondary works, as well as an introduction to loyalist literature, see the notes which accompany this study.

ABBREVIATIONS

Works frequently referred to in the Notes are abbreviated as follows:

Adams	L.H. Butterfield et al., eds., *The Adams Papers, Diary and Autobiography of John Adams* (4 vols., Cambridge, 1961)
Facs.	Benjamin Stevens, ed., *Facsimilies of Manuscripts in European Archives Relating to America, 1773–1783* (25 vols., London, 1889–98)
Franklin	Leonard Labaree et al., eds., *The Papers of Benjamin Franklin* (18 vols., New Haven, 1959–)
GP, HSP	Galloway Papers, Historical Society of Pennsylvania
GP, LC	Galloway Papers, Library of Congress
J.G.	All works by Galloway
N.J. Arch.	*New Jersey Archives*
N.Y.G.(G.)	*Gaines' New York Gazette and Weekly Mercury*

N.Y.G.(R.)	*Rivington's New York Gazetteer*
N.Y.R.G.	*New York Royal Gazette*
Pa. Arch.	*Pennsylvania Archives*
Parl. Hist.	William Cobbett, ed., *The Parliamentary History of England* (36 vols., London, 1802–20)
PH	*Pennsylvania History*
PMHB	*Pennsylvania Magazine of History and Biography*
Union	Julian P. Boyd, *Anglo-American Union: Joseph Galloway's Plans to Preserve the British Empire, 1774–1783* (Philadelphia, 1941)
WMQ	*William & Mary Quarterly*

INTRODUCTION

1. *Pennsylvania Packet* (Philadelphia), 10 June 1778; ibid., 21 June 1778; ibid., 10 June 1778.
2. Ernest H. Baldwin, "Joseph Galloway, the Loyalist Politician," *PMHB*, XXVI (1902), 440; Robert M. Calhoon, " 'I have deduced your rights': Joseph Galloway's Concept of his Role," *PH* XXXV (1968), 359; William Nelson, *The American Tory* (Boston, 1968), 54; *Franklin and Galloway*, 9–10.
3. Nelson, *The American Tory*, 48, 54, 62–63; Boyd, *Union*, 5–6.
4. Edward Tatum, ed., *The American Journal of Ambrose Serle* (Los Angeles, 1940), 171; John Vardill to William Eden, 11 Apr. 1778, *Facs.*, IV, No. 438; Boyd, *Union*, 5, 16–17; Max Savelle, "Nationalism and other Loyalties in the American Revolution," *American Historical Review*, LXVII (1962), 910.

CHAPTER 1

1. Joseph Galloway to Grace Galloway, 5 Dec. 1778, GP, HSP.
2. Thomas Balch, ed., *The Examination of Joseph Galloway, Esq., By a Committee of the House of Commons* (Philadelphia, 1855), 76n; Raymond Werner, ed., "Diary of Grace Growden Galloway," *PMHB*, LV (1931), 87, 168; Joseph Galloway to Grace Galloway, undated, GP, HSP.
3. The biographical sketch of Galloway is based on Baldwin, "Joseph Galloway," 161–64; *Union*, 17–18; [J.G.], *The Examination of Joseph Galloway . . . with Explanatory Notes* (London, 1779), 1; Nelson, *The American Tory*, 69; Thomas P. Abernathy, *Western Lands and the American Revolution* (New York, 1959), 29, 31–32; "Notes and Queries," *PMHB*, XIV (1890), 445–46; Newcomb, *Franklin and Galloway*, 11. For the complete title of all pamphlets written by Galloway, see the essay on the sources preceding the notes.

4. Theodore Thayer, *Pennsylvania Politics and the Growth of Democracy, 1740–1776* (Harrisburg, 1953), 5–7.

5. Ibid., 49–88; William Hanna, *Benjamin Franklin and Pennsylvania Politics* (Palo Alto, 1964), 4–22, 95–116; Newcomb, *Franklin and Galloway*, 17–36.

6. Newcomb, *Franklin and Galloway*, 5–17.

7. "Humphrey Scourge," *Tit for Tat, or the Score wip'd off* (Philadelphia, 1755). Galloway probably contributed essays to the 25 Mar., 22 Apr., and 17 June 1756, editions of the *Pennsylvania Journal* (Philadelphia). The essays are attributed to Galloway by Ralph Ketchum, "Benjamin Franklin and William Smith: New Light on an Old Philadelphia Quarrel," *PMHB*, LXXXVIII (1964), 143; Baldwin, "Joseph Galloway," 170; Hanna, *Benjamin Franklin*, 132; *Pa. Arch.*, 8th Ser., VI, 4386.

8. Thayer, *Pennsylvania Politics*, 49–88; Hanna, *Benjamin Franklin*, 140–53; James Hutson, *Pennsylvania Politics, 1746–1770: The Movement for Royal Government and Its Consequences* (Princeton, 1972), 41–121.

9. *Votes, Pa. Arch.*, 8th Ser., VII, 5570, 5611.

10. John Dickinson, "A Reply to the Speech of Joseph Galloway," Paul L. Ford, ed., *The Writings of John Dickinson* (Philadelphia, 1896), 112–14.

11. J.G., *The Speech of Joseph Galloway. . . .* (Philadelphia, 1764), 49–89; David Jacobson, *John Dickinson and the Revolution in Pennsylvania* (Berkeley, 1964), 13; Hanna, *Benjamin Franklin*, 149–53; *Votes, Pa. Arch.*, 8th Ser., VII, 5590–95; Newcomb, *Franklin and Galloway*, 89–90.

12. [J.G.], *A Letter to the People of Pennsylvania. . . .* (Philadelphia, 1760), 6–7.

13. Galloway to Benjamin Franklin, 16 June 1758, *Franklin*, VIII, 106; Galloway to Franklin, 16 June 1766, ibid., XIII, 318; [J.G.], *A Reply to an Address. . . .* (New York, 1775), 7; Galloway to Franklin, 16–28 Nov. 1765, *Franklin*, XII, 375; Galloway to Franklin, 13 Jan. 1766, ibid., XIII, 36–37; Galloway to Franklin, 21 June 1770, Jared Sparks, ed., *The Works of Benjamin Franklin* (10 vols., Boston, 1865), VII, 482; Galloway to Franklin, 8 Aug. 1767, *Franklin*, XIV, 229–32.

14. Galloway to Franklin, 18 July 1765, *Franklin*, XII, 219, 219n; William A. Williams, *The Contours of American History* (New York, 1961), 92–93; Hutson, *Pennsylvania Politics*, 33–34.

15. *Franklin*, XI, 394; Hutson, *Pennsylvania Politics*, 169–77; Newcomb, *Franklin and Galloway*, 87–103.

16. Jack P. Greene, "An Uneasy Connection: An Analysis of the Preconditions of the American Revolution," in Stephen G. Kurtz and James H. Hutson, eds., *Essays on the American Revolution* (Chapel Hill, 1973), 32–80.

17. Newcomb, *Franklin and Galloway*, 295.

18. *Pa. Journal*, 29 Aug. 1765.

19. Ibid. Some sketchy evidence exists that Galloway had concocted some kind of plan for imperial reform as early as 1765. The plan was never submitted to any formal body or agency and has subsequently been lost. Later he may have regretted not making some compromise proposal during the Stamp Act crisis. On the eve of the Revolution he speculated that had a compromise solution been offered in 1766 it would have gained acceptance "and the most perfect harmony would have this day subsisted between the two countries." Why Galloway did not present his plan a decade before the commencement of hostilities can only be conjectured. Possibly he hesitated because he was not a member of the Stamp Act Congress

which convened in October of 1765, and he may have felt that he lacked a suitable forum. He might have attempted to force some plan through the Pennsylvania Assembly; such an action, however, certainly would have provoked a major controversy in the colony and would have been at variance with his desire to prevent, not engender, conflict. Furthermore, he underestimated the intransigence on both sides in this early crisis. He believed each side was likely to make concessions if the impasse reached crisis proportions. Galloway to Franklin, 13 Jan. 1766, *Franklin*, XIII, 36.

20. Galloway to Franklin, 18 July 1765, *Franklin*, XII, 218.

21. *Votes, Pa. Arch.*, 8th Ser., VII, 5779–80.

22. [John Dickinson], *The Late Regulations Respecting the British Colonies on the Continent of America Considered.* . . . (Philadelphia, 1765), 31; Stephen Hopkins, *The Rights of Colonists Examined* (Providence, 1765), 21.

23. Samuel Wharton to Franklin, 13 Oct. 1765, *Franklin*, XII, 315–16; Galloway to Franklin, 20 Sept. 1765, ibid., XII, 270. See also James H. Hutson, "An Investigation of the Inarticulate: Philadelphia's White Oaks," *WMQ*, XXVIII (1971), 3–26.

24. Galloway to Franklin, 8–14 Oct. 1765, *Franklin*, XII, 305; Newcomb, *Franklin and Galloway*, 124n; Galloway to W. Franklin, 13 Sept. 1766, Franklin Papers, American Philosophical Society, I, 42; "Merchants Petition on the Stamp Act," ibid., LVII, Pt. I, No. 5; Galloway to Richard Jackson, 29 Nov. 1765, *Franklin*, XII, 389; [J.G.], *Advertisement to the Public* (Philadelphia, 1765), Broadside.

25. Galloway to Franklin, 18 July 1765, *Franklin*, XII, 217–18.

26. Jacobson, *Dickinson*, 59–60; Hutson, *Pennsylvania Politics*, 220–21.

27. *Votes, Pa. Arch.*, 8th Ser., VII, 6168; *Pennsylvania Chronicle* (Philadelphia), 25 July, 22 Aug. 1768; Newcomb, *Franklin and Galloway*, 198–207.

28. Franklin to Galloway, 12 Apr. 1766, ibid., XIII, 243; Franklin to Galloway, 13 June 1767, ibid., XIV, 182–84; Franklin to Galloway, 1 Dec. 1767, ibid., XIV, 331; Franklin to Galloway, 3 Nov. 1773, Sparks, *Works of Franklin*, VIII, 96; Franklin to Galloway, 6 Apr. 1773, John Bigelow, ed., *The Works of Benjamin Franklin* (12 vols., New York, 1904), VI, 105; [J.G.], *A Letter from Cicero to the Rt. Hon. Lord Viscount H—E.* . . . (London, 1781), 5.

29. Hutson, *Pennsylvania Politics*, 203–28; Galloway to Franklin, 17 Oct. 1768, *Franklin*, XV, 231.

30. [William Goddard], *The Partnership; or the History of the Rise and Progress of the Pennsylvania Chronicle* (Philadelphia, 1770), 16, 65–72; *Pa. Chronicle*, 16–23 Sept. 1771. For a more detailed discussion see Arthur M. Schlesinger, "Politics, Propaganda and the Philadelphia Press, 1767–1770," *PMHB*, LX (1936), 309–22.

31. *Franklin*, XIII, 447n; Galloway to Franklin, Oct. 1767, ibid., XIV, 276; Newcomb, *Franklin and Galloway*, 203.

32. Franklin to Galloway, 2 Dec. 1772, Bigelow, *Works of Franklin*, V, 399.

33. Franklin to Galloway, 6 Jan. 1773, ibid., VI, 64.

34. Boyd, *Union*, 18–19.

35. Newcomb, *Franklin and Galloway*, 222–23.

36. Galloway to Jackson, 10 Aug. 1774, Jack P. Greene, ed., *Colonies to Nation, 1763–1789* (New York, 1967), 239–40.

37. See Oliver Kuntzleman, *Joseph Galloway, Loyalist* (Philadelphia, 1941), 103–7.

38. Galloway to Jackson, 10 Aug. 1774, Greene, *Colonies to Nation*, 240.

39. Franklin to Galloway, 1 Dec. 1767, Sparks, *Works of Franklin*, VII, 370; Franklin to Galloway, 3 Nov. 1773, ibid., VIII, 96; Franklin to Galloway, 9 Jan. 1769, Carl Van Doren, ed., *Benjamin Franklin's Autobiographical Writings* (New York, 1945), 188; Verner Crane, *Benjamin Franklin: Englishman and American* (Baltimore, 1936), 135–36; Franklin to Galloway, 8 Nov. 1766, *Franklin*, XII, 488; Galloway to Franklin, 18 July 1765, ibid., XII, 218–19; Franklin to Galloway, 6 Jan. 1777, Bigelow, *Works of Franklin*, VI, 64.

40. John A. Neuenschwander, *The Middle Colonies and the Coming of the American Revolution* (Port Washington, N.Y., 1973), 28–37; Peter Force, comp., *American Archives . . .* , 4th Ser. (Washington, D.C., 1837–53), 2d Ser., I, 486.

41. W.C. Ford et al., eds., *Journals of the Continental Congress, 1774–1789* (34 vols., Washington, 1904–37), I, 26–29; *Adams*, II, 121–23, 133–35.

42. Ford, *Journals Cont. Cong.*, I, 31–40, 43.

43. [J.G.], *A Candid Examination of the Mutual Claims of Great Britain And the Colonies. . . .* (New York, 1775), 53–54.

44. Ibid., 51; *Adams*, II, 142–43; Edmund C. Burnett, ed., *Letters of Members of the Continental Congress* (8 vols., Washington, 1921–36), I, 80; Thayer, *Growth of Democracy*, 161; Ford, *Journals Cont. Cong.*, I, 75–80.

45. But, as Benjamin Newcomb notes, the plan's "real rejection was by the British ministry. It was given shorter shrift in Britain that it was in America. Parliamentary approval of it would have placed the responsibility for reconciliation squarely on the rebelling colonists." See Newcomb, *Franklin and Galloway*, 295.

46. Nelson, *The American Tory*, 58; David Ammerman, *In the Common Cause: American Response to the Coercive Acts of 1774* (New York, 1975), 55, 93; Boyd, *Union*, 5–6; Calhoon, " 'I have deduced your Rights,' " 375, 378; Wallace Brown, *The Good Americans: The Loyalists in the American Revolution* (New York, 1969), 94; Calhoon, " 'I have deduced your Rights,' " 357; *Union*, 27; Nelson, *The American Tory*, 63; Newcomb, *Franklin and Galloway*, 9–10, 297; *Union*, 32; Nelson, *The American Tory*, 48.

47. [J.G.], *Historical and Political Reflections on the Rise and Progress of the American Rebellion. . . .* (London, 1780), 67, 69.

48. *Adams*, II, 121; Vardill to Eden, 11 Apr. 1778, Stevens, *Facs.*, IV, No. 438; Tatum, *Journal of Serle*, 165, 171, 173.

49. *Adams*, II, 129–30, 143; Ford, *Journals Cont. Cong.*, I, 67–73. Whereas Congress' tenth resolution deplored "the exercise of legislative power . . . by a council appointed, during pleasure, by the crown," Galloway preferred that the Upper House of the Assembly be selected by the Monarch. Galloway, however, did not discuss provincial government in his 28 September address.

50. *Adams*, II, 143; Pauline Maier, *From Resistance to Revolution: Colonial Radicals and the Development of American Opposition to Britain, 1765–1776* (New York, 1972), 228, 246; Gordon Wood, *The Creation of the American Republic, 1776–1787* (Chapel Hill, 1967), 3–90; Bernard Bailyn, *The Ideological Origins of the American Revolution* (Cambridge, 1967), 55–143.

51. John Adams to Joseph Palmer, 26 Sept. 1774, Burnett, *Letters Cont. Cong.*, I, 48; Adams to William Tudor, 29 Sept. 1774, ibid., I, 60; Adams to Tudor, 7 Oct. 1774, ibid., I, 65; *Adams*, II, 138–39.

52. Ibid., II, 121; John Dickinson to Arthur Lee, 27 Oct. 1774, Burnett, *Letters Cont. Cong.*, I, 83; *Adams*, II, 119.

53. Ibid., II, 143.

54. Ibid., II, 119, 151; Charles Francis Adams, ed., *The Works of John Adams, Second President of the United States: With a Life of the Author* (10 vols., Boston, 1856), II, 387n; *Adams*, II, 138, 148–49.

55. Franklin to Galloway, 25 Feb. 1775, Albert H. Smyth, ed., *The Writings of Benjamin Franklin* (10 vols., New York, 1905–7), VI, 311–12.

56. *Adams*, II, 138, 148–49.

57. J.G., *A Candid Examination*, 56–58; J.G., *A Reply*, 32–33.

58. *Adams*, II, 120, 138, 140.

59. "Some Letters of Joseph Galloway, 1774–1775," *PMHB*, XXI (1897), 477–84; [Thomas B. Chandler], *A Friendly Address to all Reasonable Americans* (New York, 1774), 12; J.G., *A Candid Examination*, 53–55.

60. J.G., *A Reply to an Address*, 4–5, 9, 17; J.G., *A Candid Examination*, 2, 31.

61. J.G., *A Reply to an Address*, 41; J.G., *A Candid Examination*, 27–28.

62. J.G., *A Candid Examination*, 32.

63. Ibid., 1.

64. Ibid., 62.

65. Ibid., 46; ibid., 62.

66. Ibid.

67. Galloway to W. Franklin, 28 Feb. 1775, *N.J. Arch.*, X, 573; Galloway to W. Franklin, 26 Mar. 1775, ibid., X, 584–85; *Pa. Arch.*, 4th Ser., III, 505; *Votes, Pa. Arch.*, 8th Ser., VIII, 7210–13, 7228–30, 7232–33; Newcomb, *Franklin and Galloway*, 276–77.

68. [J.G.], *Letters from Cicero to Catiline the Second* (London, 1781), 48.

69. J.G., *A Candid Examination*, 62; J.G., *The Examination of Joseph Galloway*, 55n.

CHAPTER 2

1. The foregoing is based on the standard historical appraisals of the war. In particular, see Howard Peckham, *The War for Independence: A Military History* (Chicago, 1958).

2. Wilbur Siebert, *The Loyalists of Pennsylvania* (Columbus, 1920), 22–27; Thayer, *The Growth of Democracy*, 175–97.

3. Siebert, *The Loyalists of Pennsylvania*, 30.

4. Ira D. Gruber, *The Howe Brothers and the American Revolution* (New York, 1972), 149.

5. Galloway to Thomas McKean, 7 Mar. 1793, McKean Collection, HSP, II, No. 4; Newcomb, *Franklin and Galloway*, 217–25; Tatum, *Journal of Serle*, 165, 171, 173; Peter O. Hutchinson, ed., *The Diaries and Letters of His Excellency Thomas Hutchinson, Esq.* (2 vols., London, 1884–86), II, 229.

6. Franklin to Richard Bache, 13 Sept. 1781, Van Doren, *Franklin's Autobiography*, 509–10. Some of Galloway's contemporaries suspected that he defected out of personal fear. A poet noted at the time

> Did you not in as vile and shallow way,
> Fright our poor Philadelphian, Galloway,
> Your Congress when the daring ribald

Belied, berated and bescribbled?
What ropes and halters did you send,
Terrific emblems of his end,
Till least he'd hang in more than effigy
Fled in a fog the trembling refugee?

See Edwin T. Bowden, ed., *The Satiric Poems of John Trumbull* (Austin, 1962), 161.

7. John Coleman, "Joseph Galloway and the British Occupation of Philadelphia," *PH*, XXX (1963), 272–300; Tatum, *Journal of Serle*, 165–239.

8. Galloway to the Earl of Dartmouth, 23 Jan. 1778, *Facs.*, XXIV, No. 2078; Galloway to Dartmouth, 17 June 1778, ibid., XXIV, No. 2095; J.G., *The Examination of Joseph Galloway*, 12; [J.G.], *Plain Truth: or, A Letter to the Author of Dispassionate Thoughts on the American War* (London, 1780), 16; [J.G.], *A Letter to . . . Lord Viscount H—E* (London, 1779), 2; [J.G.], *Fabricus, or Letters to the People of Great Britain* (London, 1782), 74; [J.G.], *Letters to a Nobleman, on the Conduct of the War in the Middle Colonies* (London, 1779), 20.

9. Galloway to Franklin, 13 Jan. 1765, *Franklin*, XIII, 217–18; J.G., *A Reply*, 3–4; Galloway to Dartmouth, 3 Dec. 1777, *Facs.*, XXIV, No. 2069; Galloway to Dartmouth, 23 Jan. 1778, ibid., XXIV, No. 2078; J.G., "A View of the Present Strength of America in Respect to Her Number of Fighting Men," 1778, ibid., XXIV, No. 2098.

10. Galloway to Serle, 15 Dec. 1777, ibid., XXIV, No. 2074; Galloway to Dartmouth, 3 Dec. 1777, ibid., XXIV, No. 2069; Galloway to Dartmouth, 20 Jan. 1778, ibid., XXIV, No. 2078; Galloway to Dartmouth, 4 Mar. 1778, ibid., XXIV, No. 2090; Galloway to Dartmouth, 24 Mar. 1778,. ibid., No. 2092; Galloway to Dartmouth, 17 June 1778, ibid., XXIV, No. 2095.

11. Tatum, *Journal of Serle*, 178, 179, 191; Galloway to Dartmouth, 24 Mar. 1778, *Facs.*, XXIV, No. 2092; Galloway to Dartmouth, 3 Dec. 1777, ibid., XXIV, No. 2069; Galloway to Dartmouth, 4 Mar. 1778, ibid., XXIV, No. 2090. See also J.G., *The Examination of Joseph Galloway*, 29.

12. Galloway to Serle, 15 Dec. 1777, *Facs.*, XXIV, No. 2074; Galloway to Dartmouth, 3 Dec. 1777, ibid., XXIV, No. 2069; Galloway to Dartmouth, 20 Jan. 1778, ibid., XXIV, No. 2078; Galloway, *Letters to a Nobleman*, 25; J.G., "An Account of the Number of Deserted Soldiers. . . . ," 1778, *Facs.*, XXIV, No. 2094; Galloway to Dartmouth, 20 Jan. 1778, *Facs.*, XXIV, No. 2078; J.G., *Letters to a Nobleman*, 25.

13. J.G., *The Examination of Joseph Galloway*, 70n; J.G., *Letters to a Nobleman*, 34–35; Galloway to Dartmouth, 3 Dec. 1777, *Facs.*, XXIV, No. 2069; J.G., *The Examination of Galloway*, 28–29; J.G., *Letters to a Nobleman*, 34–35; Tatum, *Journal of Serle*, 182, 192, 196.

14. J.G., *Plain Truth*, 16.

15. Christopher Ward, *The War of the Revolution* (2 vols., New York, 1952), I, 285; Douglas Southall Freeman, *George Washington* (7 vols., New York, 1948–57), IV, 533n, 622n, V, 110, 137; J.G., *The Examination of Galloway*, 30.

16. Freeman, *Washington*, IV, 338n, 382, 568; Peckham, *War for Independence*, 82; Lawrence H. Gipson, *The Coming of the Revolution, 1763–1775* (New York, 1954), 10; John C. Miller, *Origins of the American Revolution* (New York, 1943), 53; Merrill Jensen, *The Founding of a Nation: A History of the American Revolution, 1763–1776* (New York, 1968), 8.

17. General William Howe, *The Narrative of Lieut. Gen. Sir William Howe . . . to which are added, Some Observations Upon a Pamphlet Entitled, Letters to a Nobleman* (London, 1780), 41; Nelson, *The American Tory*, 92; Brown, *The Good Americans*, 226–38; Mary Beth Norton, *The British-Americans: The Loyalist Exiles in England, 1774–1789* (Boston, 1972), 37–39.

18. Coleman, "Galloway and the British Occupation of Philadelphia," 274–76, 287–94.

19. Tatum, *Journal of Serle*, 296–300.

20. J.G., *Plain Truth*, 17; J.G., "Reasons against abandoning the city of Philadelphia. . . . ," *Facs.*, XXIV, No. 2096.

21. Elizabeth Galloway to Grace Galloway, 9 Oct. 1778, GP, HSP.

22. Werner, "Diary of Grace Galloway," 57, 88, 167, 177–78; Grace Galloway to Elizabeth Galloway, Undated [1778?], GP, LC.

23. Quoted in Solomon Lutnick, *The American Revolution and the British Press, 1775–1783* (Columbia, Mo., 1967), 58–59, 108; Dora Mae Clark, *British Opinion and the American Revolution* (New Haven, 1930), 112–45; Charles Ritcheson, *British Politics and the American Revolution* (Norman, Okla., 1954), 269–70; Weldon Brown, *Empire or Independence: Failure of Reconciliation* (New York, 1941), 249–52.

24. Walter Clark, *Josiah Tucker: Economist* (New York, 1902), 187–90; Klaus Knorr, *British Colonial Theories, 1570–1850* (Toronto, 1963), 117–52; Edwin Cannon, ed., *An Inquiry into the Nature and Causes of the Wealth of Nations, by Adam Smith* (New York, 1937), 560–81.

25. [John Cartwright], *American Independence and the Interest and Glory of Great Britain* (Philadelphia, 1776), 33–36, 44–47, 147.

26. Lutnick, *Revolution and the British Press*, 125. Maudit's pamphlet, *A Hand bill advocating American Independence, inspired by the English ministry* (London, 1778), has been the subject of considerable historical debate. For some time the pamphlet was thought to be the inspiration of the opposition faction in Britain. The leading exponent of this position was Worthington C. Ford, "Parliament and the Howes," Massachusetts Historical Society, *Proceedings*, XLIV (1910–11), 120–43. More recent studies, such as that by Lutnick and Robert Taylor, "Israel Maudit," *New England Quarterly*, XXIV (1951), 208–30, indicated that Maudit was acting in behalf of the ministry. It is possible, as Taylor suggests, that Maudit was backed by Germain, a minister anxious to avoid charges of responsibility for the catastrophe at Saratoga.

27. Lutnick, *Revolution and the British Press*, 126–29.

28. Norton, *The British-Americans*, 162–67.

29. [J.G.], *Cool Thoughts on the Consequences to Great Britain of American Independence. . . .* (London, 1780), 2–3, 13–15, 18–21, 25–27, 47–53.

30. Ibid., 33–34, 45, 64–65; J.G., *Fabricus*, 2–4; J.G., *Cool Thoughts*, 13–14.

31. Ibid., 69.

32. Ibid., 5–7, 12–14, 33, 52.

33. J.G., *Plain Truth*, 11–12.

34. Ibid., 13; J.G., *A Letter to the Right Honourable*, 46; J.G., *Fabricus*, 5, 25, 61.

35. J.G., *Letters to a Nobleman*, 26, 49, 74, 76, 87; Galloway to Dartmouth, 3 Dec. 1777, *Facs.*, XXIV, No. 2069; J.G., *Plain Truth*, 19; J.G., *The Examination of Galloway*, 70n.

36. Galloway to General Burgoyne, c. 1780, GP, LC.

37. J.G., *Fabricus*, 60–63.

38. J.G., *A Letter to the Right Honourable*, 14–37.

39. J.G., *A Letter from Cicero*, 3, 12–15; J.G., *Letters from Cicero to Catiline*, 34–35; [J.G.], *A Reply to the Observations of Lieut. Gen. Sir William Howe*. . . . (London, 1780), 120.

40. J.G., *Plain Truth*, 14–15; Galloway to Dartmouth, 20 Jan. 1778, *Facs.*, XXIV, No. 2078.

41. Galloway to Burgoyne, c. 1780, GP, LC; J.G., *Letters to a Nobleman*, 51, 57; J.G., *Fabricus*, 7–8.

42. Galloway to Lord Howe, c. 1780, GP, LC.

43. J.G., *Letters to a Nobleman*, 42; J.G., *Plain Truth*, 18; J.G., *A Letter to the Right Honourable*, 35; J.G., *A Reply to the Observations*, 68; Claude H. Van Tyne, *The Loyalists in the American Revolution* (New York, 1970), 161.

44. J.G., *Letters to a Nobleman*, 2–5, 36–37; Lutnick, *Revolution and the British Press*, 121–22; Alan Valantine, *Lord North* (2 vols., Norman, Okla., 1967), II, 38–40; G.H. Guttridge, *English Whiggism and the American Revolution* (Berkeley, 1963), 108; J.G., *A Reply to the Observations*, 11–12.

45. Galloway to Grace Galloway, 21 Mar. 1777, GP, LC; Galloway to Burgoyne, c. 1780, ibid. Galloway's views on the use of terrorism have been echoed recently by a British military historian who suggested that fewer prisoners could have been taken and that "partisans not in uniform [might have been] executed out of hand." See Piers Mackesy, "British Strategy in the War of Independence," *The Yale Review*, LII (1963), 539–637.

46. J.G., *Fabricus*, 4–15.

47. Galloway to W. Franklin, 3 Sept. 1774, *N.J. Arch.*, X, 476–77; Galloway to Lord George Germain, 18 Mar. 1779, *Union*, 116–18; Galloway to Charles Jenkinson, c. 1780, ibid., 127–56; Galloway Plan of Union, ibid., 175; J.G., *A Reply to an Address*, 7; Galloway to Franklin, 16–28 Nov. 1765, *Franklin*, XII, 375; Galloway to Franklin, 13 Jan. 1766, ibid., XIII, 36–37; Galloway to Franklin, 21 June 1770, ibid., XVII, 177–78; J.G., *Plain Truth*, 48–49.

48. J.G., *Fabricus*, 7–8.

49. Eric Robson, *The American Revolution: In Its Political and Military Aspects, 1763-1783* (New York, 1966), 97, 101, 127; Peckham, *The War for Independence*, 134; Paul Smith, *Loyalists and Redcoats: A Study in British Revolutionary Policy* (Chapel Hill, 1964), 79–99; William B. Willcox, "Sir Henry Clinton: Paralysis of Command," in George A. Billias, ed., *George Washington's Opponents: British Generals and Admirals in the American Revolution* (New York, 1969), 84–85.

50. Quoted in Maldyn Jones, "Sir William Howe: Conventional Strategist," in Billias, *George Washington's Opponents*, 56; see also Robson, *The American Revolution*, 160.

51. Ford, "Parliament and the Howes," 120–44; Charles F. Adams, "Contemporary Opinion on the Howes," Mass Hist. Soc., *Proceedings*, XLIV (1910–11), 94–120; Gerald S. Brown, ed., *Reflections on a Pamphlet Intitled "A Letter to the Right Hon. Lord H—E," by Admiral Lord Howe* (Ann Arbor, 1959), 1–15.

52. *Parl. Hist.*, XX, 331, 393, 698, ibid., XX, 678–80, 689, 702.

53. Ibid., XX, 682, 692.

54. Ibid., XX, 683–86, 693, 696–99.

55. Ibid., XX, 331–32, 340–42, 711–12, 720, 756, 814.

56. Ibid., XX, 805, 853.

57. Worthington C. Ford, "The Maudit Pamphlets," Mass. Hist. Soc., *Proceedings*, XLIV (1910–11), 174; J.G., *The Examination of Galloway*, 47–64, 79. Also see *Parl. Hist.*, XXII, 338–57, as well as XXIII, 374–412, 439–517, for frequent allegations that the loyalists were pensioned by the ministry in return for their political support. Galloway had accepted pay while in the service of the British armed forces in America—he received £1070 while an official in occupied Philadelphia—and he admitted to the Commons that he had received an additional "small pittance." Following the war he and approximately two thousand other loyalists received a pension from the British government, but no evidence exists that Galloway was paid by the ministry, or by individual ministers, to publicly urge a continuation of hostilities. Nor is it likely that he required the inducement of a pension to remain an active loyalist. See Coleman, "Galloway and the British Occupation of Philadelphia," 289; J.G., *The Examination of Galloway*, 79. In addition to Galloway, scores of loyalists received pensions from Britain before the war ended. In fact, by 1783 Britain was spending about £40,200 each year on temporary pensions to loyalist refugees. See Van Tyne, *The Loyalists in the American Revolution*, 254–55, and Lewis Einstein, *Divided Loyalties: Americans in London During the War for Independence* (Boston, 1933), 229, 235, 240, 264.

58. *Parl. Hist.*, XXII, 1038–39, 1043; J.G., *The Examination of Galloway*, 60–73; Hutchinson, *Diary and Letters* of Hutchinson, II, 261; Adams, "Contemporary Opinion on the Howes," 114.

59. *Parl. Hist.*, XX, 759, 818.

60. Ibid., XX, 836–53, 905, 915.

61. Ford, "Parliament and the Howes," 139–41.

62. *Parl. Hist.*, XXII, 726, 829, 1031–32, 1071, 1085, 1089; ibid., XXII, 1038–39, 1043–44, 1089, 1101, and XXIII, 565.

63. Ibid., XXIII, 374–412.

64. Ibid., XXIII, 439–517.

65. [J.G.], *Observations on the Fifth Article of the Treaty with America....* (London, 1783), 8–12, 17.

66. [J.G.], *The Claim of the Loyalists Revived and Maintained....* (London, 1788), 11, 22–24, 57–100, 113–14.

67. Baldwin, "Joseph Galloway," 438, 438n.

68. Norton, *The British-Americans*, 60, 238; Kuntzleman, *Joseph Galloway*, 161; Galloway to McKean, 7 Mar. 1793, McKean Coll., II, No. 4, HSP.

69. Kuntzleman, *Joseph Galloway*, 165.

CHAPTER 3

1. Bailyn, *The Ideological Origins*.

2. Gordon Wood, "Rhetoric and Reality in the American Revolution," *WMQ*, XXII (1966), 3–32.

3. Bailyn, *Ideological Origins*, 57, 59, 67, 70. See also Wood, *Creation of the American Republic*, and Maier, *From Resistance to Revolution*.

4. Bailyn, *Ideological Origins*, 94–95; Maier, *From Resistance to Revolution*, 161.

5. J.G., *A Letter to the People*, 4–7.

6. Ibid.

7. Ibid., 3; J.G., *Cool Thoughts*, 4; ibid., 4.

8. J.G., *A Candid Examination*, 23, 34–36; [J.G.], *Political Reflections on the Late Colonial Governments....* (London, 1783), 2, 4–5, 7–8, 23; J.G., *A Candid Examination*, 13, 23; J.G., *Political Reflections*, 3, 12.

9. J.G., *Historical and Political Reflections*, 124; J.G., *Political Reflections*, 8, 109; J.G., *The Speech of Joseph Galloway*, 27; Galloway to Franklin, 10 Mar. 1768, *Franklin*, XV, 71–72.

10. J.G., *Political Reflections*, 2–3; J.G., "Arguments on Both Sides, in the Dispute Between Great Britain and her Colonies," *N.J. Arch.*, 1st Ser., X, 478–79; Galloway to Jenkinson, c. 1780, *Union*, 133.

11. Galloway to Jenkinson, ibid., 134.

12. J.G., *A Candid Examination*, 40, 42; J.G., *Historical and Political Reflections*, 75–76; J.G., *A Reply to an Address*, 13–15.

13. *Adams*, II, 130; J.G., "Arguments on Both Sides," *N.J. Arch.*, 1st Ser., X, 485–86; J.G., *A Candid Examination*, 39–40.

14. J.G., *A Letter to the People of Pennsylvania*, 3–4.

15. J.G., *Political Reflections*, 3–5, 7–8.

16. Galloway to Jenkinson, c. 1780, *Union*, 146, 153; J.G., *A Candid Examination*, 32–33; Galloway to Franklin, 23 Nov. 1764, *Franklin*, XI, 467–68; J.G., *Historical and Political Reflections*, 42–43, 66–67.

17. Wood, *The Creation of the American Republic*, 46–70; J.G., *A Candid Examination*, 1, 29, 32–33, 62.

18. J.G., *A Letter to the People of Pennsylvania*, 3–5; J.G., *The Examination of Galloway*, 9n; *Pa. Chronicle*, 15 Aug. 1768; Galloway to Franklin, 18 July 1765, *Franklin*, XII, 217–18; *Pa. Journal*, 29 Aug. 1765; J.G., *Political Reflections*, 203–4.

19. J.G., *A Candid Examination*, 32–33.

20. J.G., *Political Reflections*, 9–10, 14; J.G., *The Speech of Joseph Galloway*, 34; *Pa. Chronicle*, 15 Aug. 1768; J.G., *Historical and Political Reflections*, 113.

21. J.G., *Political Reflections*, 8, 10, 14; J.G., *The Speech of Joseph Galloway*, 34; *Pa. Chronicle*, 15 Aug. 1768.

22. J.G., *Political Reflections*, 16; J.G., *A Candid Examination*, 7, 34–35.

23. J.G., *A Candid Examination*, 7; ibid., 4–5. Galloway is directly quoting Burlamaqui.

24. J.G., *Political Reflections*, 17–19.

25. Ibid., 26–27.

26. Ibid., 28–33.

27. Galloway to Jenkinson, *Union*, 136.

28. *Pa. Chronicle*, 15 Aug. 1768.

29. J.G., *Political Reflections*, 8–9, 56–57; J.G., *Historical and Political Reflections*, 45–46; J.G., *Plain Truth*, 48–49.

30. J.G., *A Candid Examination*, 1, 34, 39–40, 59.

CHAPTER 4

1. Wood, *Creation of the American Republic*, 350–51; Franklin to W. Franklin, 13 Mar. 1768, *Franklin*, XV, 75–76.

2. Wood, *Creation of the American Republic*, 344–54; Bailyn, *Ideological Origins*, 198–229.

3. *Pa. Journal*, 7 Mar. 1775.

4. Ford, *Journals Cont. Cong.*, I, 67–73.

5. J.G., *A Candid Examination*, 3–4.

6. Ibid., 4–5, 24; J.G., *Political Reflections*, 30–31.

7. J.G., *A Candid Examination*, 7, 9; J.G., *A Reply to an Address*, 18.

8. J.G., *Political Reflections*, 44–47; J.G., *A Candid Examination*, 12, 15; J.G., *A Reply to an Address*, 12.

9. J.G., *A Candid Examination*, 10–13; ibid., 10–11, 17–18; J.G., *A Reply to an Address*, 16; J.G., *Political Reflections*, 69–238.

10. J.G., *A Candid Examination*, 16–17, 20.

11. J.G., *A Reply to an Address*, 9, 15, 20.

12. *Adams*, II, 129–30, 140–41.

13. J.G., *A Candid Examination*, 6.

14. Ibid., 39–40; J.G., *A Reply to an Address*, 10; *Adams*, II, 129–30.

15. J.G., *A Candid Examination*, 42; J.G., *Cool Thoughts*, 17; J.G., *A Letter to the People*, 12–39; Galloway to Franklin, 17 Oct. 1768, *Franklin*, XV, 231; Galloway to Franklin, 23 Nov. 1764, ibid., XI, 468.

16. J.G., *A Reply to an Address*, 9; J.G., *Political Reflections*, 26, 30–31, 50, 70, 76–77, 104.

17. Ibid., 50–53, 228–38.

18. Ibid., 60.

19. Ibid., 97–105; [J.G.], *A True and Impartial State of the Province of Pennsylvania* (Philadelphia, 1759), 30; *Votes, Pa. Arch.*, 8th Ser., VII, 5590–95; [J.G.], *To the Freeholders, and other Electors of Assembly-men for Pennsylvania* (Philadelphia, 1765), 1; [J.G.], *An Address to the Freeholders and Inhabitants of the Province of Pennsylvania* (Philadelphia, 1764), 8.

20. J.G., *Political Reflections*, 99; Galloway to Franklin, 10 Mar. 1768, *Franklin*, XV, 71–72.

21. J.G., *A Candid Examination*, 41–42; J.G., *A Letter to the People of Pennsylvania*, 35–36.

22. See Richard Van Alstyne, *The Rising American Empire* (Chicago, 1965), 1–27; Richard Van Alstyne, *Genesis of American Nationalism* (Walthorn, Mass., 1970), 51–53; Max Savelle, *The Seeds of Liberty* (Seattle, 1965), 557–60.

23. Louis B. Wright, ed., *An Essay Upon the Government of the English Plantations on the Continent of America* (San Marino, Cal., 1954), 20–54. For other plans of empire, see Richard Koebner, *Empire* (Cambridge, 1961); Jack Greene, "Martin Blander's Blueprint for a Colonial Union," *WMQ*, XVII (1960), 516–30; Roy Lokken, "Sir William Keith's Theory of the British Empire," *The Historian*, XXV (1963), 403–18; Richard Frothingham, *The Rise of the Republic of the United States* (Boston, 1910), 109–20; Albert Hart and Edward Channing, ed., *American History Leaflets*, No. 14 (March 1894); Knorr, *British Colonial Theories*.

24. Richard Van Alstyne, *Empire and Independence* (New York, 1965), 12, 45–46; Koebner, *Empire*, 105–43; Charles Mullett, "English Imperial Thinking, 1764–1783," *Political Science Quarterly*, XLV (1930), 550–58.

25. [Thomas Pownall], *The Administration of the Colonies* (London, 1768), 34–35; also see G.H. Guttridge, "Thomas Pownall's The Administration of the Colonies: The Six Editions," *WMQ*, XXVI (1969), 31–46.

26. [Francis Bernard], *Select Letters on the Trade and Government of America* (London, 1774), vi., 44, 71–83.

27. [Benjamin Franklin], *Observations Concerning the Increase of Mankind*

(Boston, 1755), *Franklin*, IV, 225–34; Franklin to John Hughes, 9 Aug. 1765, ibid., XII, 234; Franklin to James Parker, 20 Mar. 1751, ibid., IV, 119; Franklin to William Shirley, 22 Dec. 1754, ibid., V, 449–50.

28. In 1775 Galloway publicly demonstrated the lack of similarity in his plan and that of Franklin. Unlike Franklin's proposal, the Galloway plan would have created an American branch of Parliament and resolved the question of imperial sovereignty. See the *Pennsylvania Gazette* (Philadelphia), 26 Apr. 1775. Furthermore, as Robert Calhoon notes, Franklin's population thesis had a much greater influence on Galloway than did the Albany Plan. See Calhoon, " 'I have deduced your Rights,' " 367.

29. J.G., *Plain Truth*, 2–3; J.G., *A Reply to an Address*, 9.

30. Galloway to Jackson, 10 Aug. 1774, Greene, *Colonies to Nation*, 240; Galloway to Samuel Verplanck, 17 Aug. 1775, *PMHB*, XXI, 484; *Pa. Chronicle*, 25 July 1768; J.G., *Historical and Political Reflections*, 4; *Pa. Journal*, 29 Aug. 1765; J.G., *A Candid Examination*, 1.

31. J.G., *Fabricus*, 65.

32. J.G., *Cool Thoughts*, 17; J.G., *A Reply to an Address*, 7; J.G., *Fabricus*, 65.

33. Galloway to Franklin, 16 June 1758, *Franklin*, VIII, 106; Galloway to Franklin, 23 May 1766, ibid., XIII, 285; J.G., *Historical and Political Reflections*, 21, 59–60; J.G., *Letters from Cicero*, 20–23, 34–35, 42–43; J.G., *A Letter from Cicero*, 2–3; Galloway to Jenkinson, c. 1780, *Union*, 158; Galloway to Jackson, 10 Aug. 1774, Greene, *Colonies to Nation*, 239; Galloway to Franklin, 16–28 Nov. 1765, *Franklin*, XII, 375; Galloway to Franklin, 16–28 Nov. 1765, ibid., XII, 376.

34. Galloway Plan of Union, c. 1780, *Union*, 127; J.G., *Historical and Political Reflections*, 117.

35. Calhoon, " 'I have deduced your Rights,' " 365–78.

36. For a more complete discussion of several possible constitutional revisions see Randolph Adams, *Political Ideas of the American Revolution* (New York, 1958), 42–85.

37. Galloway to Jenkinson, c. 1780, *Union*, 128, 153.

38. All of Galloway's plans are printed in *Union*, 105–56, 173–77. Professor Boyd attributes a 1785 plan of union to Galloway, but it now seems likely that the scheme came from the pen of Jonathan Sewall, a loyalist from Massachusetts. See William Nelson, "The Last Hope of the American Loyalists," *Canadian Historical Review*, XXXII (1951), 22–42, and Carol Berkin, *Jonathan Sewall: Odyssey of an American Loyalist* (New York, 1974), 160n.

39. Galloway to W. Franklin, 3 Sept. 1774, *N.J. Arch.*, 1st Ser., X, 476–77; Galloway Plan of Union, 1779, *Union*, 116–18. In spite of his persistent attachment to bicameralism, Galloway recommended a unicameral American congress in his formal presentation to the First Continental Congress. See *Union*, 112–14; Galloway to W. Franklin, 3 Sept. 1774, *N.J. Arch.*, 1st Ser., X, 476–77; Galloway to Lord Germain, 18 Mar. 1779, Stopford-Sackville Collection, Clements Library.

40. Galloway to Jenkinson, c. 1780, *Union*, 137, 154; Galloway Plan of Union, 1788, ibid., 173; Galloway Plan of Union, 1788, ibid., 173; Galloway to Jenkinson, c. 1780, ibid., 137, 142; J.G., *Candid Examination*, 53–55.

41. Galloway to Jenkinson, c. 1780, *Union*, 142.

42. J.G., *A Candid Examination*, 53–55.

43. J.G., *A Reply to an Address*, 7; Galloway to Franklin, 16–28 Nov. 1765, *Franklin*, XII, 375; Galloway to Franklin, 13 Jan. 1766, ibid., XIII, 36–37;

Galloway to Franklin, 21 June 1770, Sparks, *Works of Franklin*, VII, 482; Galloway Plan of Union, 1788, *Union*, 175.

44. Galloway Plan of Union, 1788, *Union*, 174; Galloway to Jenkinson, c. 1780, ibid., 134–36, 141–42, 147–48, 150; Galloway Plan of Union, 1788, ibid., 175–76; J.G., *Political Reflections*, 54–55; Galloway to Germain, Stopford-Sackville Coll., Clements Library.

45. Galloway Plan of Union, 1788, *Union*, 176.

46. Galloway to Jenkinson, c. 1780, ibid., 143–44, 154; Galloway Plan of Union, 1788, ibid., 175–76; J.G., *Political Reflections*, 54–55.

47. J.G., *Political Reflections*, 8–9, 56–57; J.G., *Historical and Political Reflections*, 45–46; J.G., *Plain Truth*, 48–49.

48. J.G., *Plain Truth*, 48–49.

CHAPTER 5

1. Bernard Bailyn, *The Ordeal of Thomas Hutchinson* (Cambridge, 1974), 384, 386. For an assessment of loyalist historians see Lawrence H. Leder, ed., *The Colonial Legacy: Loyalist Historians* (12 vols., New York, 1971), I; Norton, *The British-Americans*, 130–54.

2. J.G., *Historical and Political Reflections*, 2.

3. Ibid.

4. Ibid.

5. J.G., *Plain Truth*, 42, 45.

6. Galloway to Jackson, 20 Mar. 1777, *Facs.*, XXIV, No. 2051; Galloway to Jenkinson, c. 1780, *Union*, 145–46; J.G., *Political Reflections*, 60, 203–4; J.G., *Historical and Political Reflections*, 19–21.

7. Galloway to Franklin, 27 Feb. 1765, Sparks, *Works of Franklin*, VII, 285–87; Galloway to Franklin, 17 Oct. 1768, *Franklin*, XV, 230–31.

8. J.G., *Political Reflections*, 113–14, 179–82.

9. J.G., *Historical and Political Reflections*, 19–21, 24–30, 37–38, 40, 42; Galloway to Franklin, 13 Jan. 1766, *Franklin*, XIII, 36.

10. J.G., *Historical and Political Reflections*, 46–47.

11. Ibid., 12, 54–57; J.G., *Political Reflections*, 251–53.

12. J.G., *Historical and Political Reflections*, 60–61; J.G., *A Reply to the Observations*, 115–16; J.G., *Fabricus*, 44; J.G., *Letters from Cicero*.

13. J.G., *Historical and Political Reflections*, 5–9.

14. J.G., *Political Reflections*, 249–50; Galloway to Jackson, 10 Aug. 1774, Greene, *Colonies to Nation*, 240; *Adams*, II, 141; J.G., *Historical and Political Reflections*, 46–47.

15. Galloway to Jackson, 10 Aug. 1774, Greene, *Colonies to Nation*, 240.

16. J.G., *Historical and Political Reflections*, 10–11, 23.

17. Ibid., 14–15.

18. Ibid., 17–18, 21, 57. Galloway defended one aspect of the Coercive Acts. The Massachusetts Government Act, he insisted, strengthened the balanced nature of government in that colony; the ministry should now "proceed in the work till every Colony charter is made conformable to the true fundamental principles of a mixed monarchy." See ibid., 21.

19. Ibid., 64–65.

20. Ibid., 66–67, 91–92.
21. Ibid., 66, 69–70, 81, 89–93, 95.
22. Ibid., 107–8.
23. See Chapter 2.

CHAPTER 6

1. Newcomb, *Franklin and Galloway.*
2. Norton, *The British-Americans*, 8; Brown, *The Good Americans*, 44–81.
3. E.A. Jones, ed., "Letter of David Colden, Loyalist, 1783," *American Historical Review*, XXV (1919), 83; Leonard Labaree, *Conservatism in Early American History* (New York, 1948), 109, 112; Jonathan Boucher, *Reminiscences of an American Loyalist* (Port Washington, N.Y., 1967), 12, 119; [Jonathan Boucher], *A View of the Causes and Consequences of the American Revolution in Thirteen Discourses* (London, 1797), 514n; [Charles Inglis], *The Christian Soldier's Duty Briefly Delineated in a Sermon* (New York, 1777), 12–13; Brown, *The Good Americans*, 63.
4. Labaree, *Conservatism*, 75, 100; [Jonathan Boucher], *A Letter from a Virginian, to the Members of Congress* (New York, 1774), 9; *Pennsylvania Packet* (Philadelphia), 22 May 1775; Boucher, *A View of the Causes*, 511; Douglas Adair and John Schultz, eds., *Peter Oliver's Origin and Progress of the American Rebellion* (San Marino, Cal., 1961), 4–8; *Massachusetts Gazette and Boston News Letter*, 27 Oct. 1774; *N.Y.G.(G.)*, 25 July 1774.
5. Boucher, *A Letter from a Virginian*, 8, 15; [Harrison Gray], *A Few Remarks upon some of the Votes and Resolutions of the Continental Congress* (Boston, 1775), 3; Labaree, *Conservatism*, 75, 100.
6. *N.Y.G.(R.)*, 2 Dec. 1773; Boucher, *A View of the Causes*, 363; [John Jacob Zubly], *A Sermon on American Affairs* (Philadelphia, 1775), 6–7.
7. [Samuel Seabury], *The Congress Canvassed. . . .* (New York, 1774), 15.
8. [Thomas Bradbury Chandler], *A Friendly Address to all Reasonable Americans* (New York, 1774), 3; *N.Y.R.G.*, 7 Oct. 1778; [Charles Inglis], *The True Interest of America Impartially stated, in certain strictures on a pamphlet intitled Common Sense* (Philadelphia, 1776), 17–18. (The *New York Royal Gazette* was also published by James Rivington.) See also Labaree, *Conservatism*, 133–34.
9. Ibid., 116; ibid., 140; *N.Y.R.G.*, 7 Oct. 1778; [James Chalmers], *Plain Truth . . . Containing Remarks on a Late Pamphlet, entitled Common Sense* (Philadelphia, 1776), 8; Chandler, *A Friendly Address*, 5; Boucher, *A View of the Causes*, 520-23; Wood, *Creation of the American Republic*, 66–67; *N.Y.R.G.*, 14 Oct. 1778; Labaree, *Conservatism*, 66; Chalmers, *Plain Truth*, 10–11; Berkin, *Jonathan Sewall*, 112–13.
10. "Letters of Rev. Jonathan Boucher," *Maryland Historical Magazine*, VIII (1913), 183–84; James Hosmer, *The Life of Thomas Hutchinson* (Boston, 1896), 167; Adair and Schutz, *Peter Oliver's Origin and Progress*, 14–19.
11. [Isaac Hunt], *The Political Family; or . . . the Reciprocal Advantages, which flow from an uninterrupted union. . . .* (Philadelphia, 1775), 8–9; Boucher, *A Letter*, 10; Hosmer, *Life of Hutchinson*, 363; William Sabine, ed., *Historical Memoirs of William Smith* (New York, 1956), 271.
12. [Daniel Leonard], *The Origins of the American Contest with Great-Britain. . . .* (Boston, 1775), 47–48; Adams, *Works*, IV, 37–38, 46–48, 122–23.

13. [Thomas Chandler], *The American Querist* (New York, 1775), 7–13; [Martin Howard], *A Letter from a Gentleman at Halifax to his Friend in Rhode Island. . . .* (Newport, 1765), 8–9; [Martin Howard], *A Defence of the Letter from a Gentleman at Halifax. . . .* (Newport, 1765), 13; Sabine, *Memoirs of Smith*, 272; L.F.S. Upton, *The Loyal Whig: William Smith of New York and Quebec* (Toronto, 1969), 1, 5–6.

14. [Jonathan Sewall], *A Cure for the Spleen. Or Amusement for a Winter's Evening. . . .* (Boston, 1775), 15; Chandler, *A Friendly Address*, 12–13.

15. [Samuel Seabury], *A View of the Controversy between Great Britain and her Colonies. . . .* (New York, 1774), 9–10, 16; Leonard, *The Origins*, 79; Hosmer, *Life of Hutchinson*, 367; Hunt, *The Political Family*, 6–7.

16. Seabury, *A View of the Controversy*, 14–15.

17. Leonard, *The Origins*, 44; Howard, *A Letter from a Gentleman*, 12–13; Hosmer, *Life of Hutchinson*, 355–56; [William Knox], *The Controversy Between Great Britain and her Colonies Reviewed: The Several Plans of the Colonies* (Boston, 1769), 54–55.

18. Howard, *A Letter from a Gentleman*, 7–12; Howard, *A Defence*, 12–13.

19. [Daniel Dulany], *Considerations on the Propriety of Imposing Taxes in the British Colonies, For the Purpose of Raising a Revenue, by Act of Parliament* (Annapolis, 1765), 10–11, 29–31.

20. Bernard Bailyn, ed., *Pamphlets of the American Revolution* (Cambridge, 1965), 605.

21. Leonard, *The Origins*, 41; Chandler, *A Friendly Address*, 5.

22. *N.Y.G.(R.)*, 6 May and 20 May 1775; Howard, *A Defence*, 20; Leonard, *The Origins*, 44; Hunt, *The Political Family*, 6–7; Hosmer, *Life of Hutchinson*, 367.

23. [Anon.], *Some Seasonable Observations and remarks upon the state of our controversy with Great Britain; and on the Proceedings of the Continental Congress* (Boston, 1775), 11–12; *Pa. Gazette*, 18 Jan. 1775; Leonard, *The Origins*, 59; [John Jacob Zubly], *The Stamp Act Repealed. A Sermon Preached in the meeting at Savannah, in Georgia, June 25th, 1766* (Savannah, 1766); Sewall, *A Cure for the Spleen*, 25; Seabury, *A View of the Controversy*, 14; E.B. O'Callaghan and B. Fernow, eds., *Documents Relative to the Colonial History of the State of New York* (15 vols., Albany, 1856–87), VIII, 217.

24. Hunt, *The Political Family*, 14; *N.Y.G.(G.)*, 19 Sept. 1774; Leonard, *The Origins*, 59, 117; *Pa. Gazette*, 15 Feb. 1775.

25. Boucher, *Reminiscences*, 133; Leonard, *The Origins*, 60–63; [Henry Barry], *The Advantages which America derives from Her commerce, connexion and Dependence on Britain* (New York, 1775), 10; *Virginia Gazette* (Williamsburg), 27 Apr. 1776.

26. [William Knox], *The Interest of the Merchants and Manufacturers of Great Britain* (London, 1775), 20; Chalmers, *Plain Truth*, 55–57; Hunt, *The Political Family*, 6–7; Barry, *The Advantages Which America Derives*, 5–10; Robert M. Calhoon, "William Smith Junior's Alternative to the American Revolution," *WMQ*, XXII (1965), 112; Leonard, *The Origins*, 103.

27. *Pa. Packet*, 2 Jan. 1775; Upton, *The Loyal Whig*, 105; Sewall, *A Cure for the Spleen*, 9.

28. Leonard, *The Origins*, 101–3.

29. [Thomas Bradbury Chandler], *What Think Ye of the Congress Now?* (New York, 1775), 12, 15–16; [Anon.], *Some Seasonable Observations*, 13; *Massachusetts Gazette*, 30 Mar. 1775; *N.Y.G.(R.)*, 2 Dec. 1773; Boucher, *A Letter*, 24.

30. W. Franklin to Galloway, 12 Mar. 1775, *N.J. Arch.*, 1st Ser., X, 578–79; The North ministry proposed in the spring of 1775 to cease taxing any colony which voluntarily raised sufficient revenue to meet the expenses of normal governmental operation and which, in addition, raised appropriations for the purpose of military defense and surrendered the sum to Parliament. *Parl. Hist.*, XVIII, 305–36; *N.Y.G.(G.)*, 25 July 1776; *N.Y.G.(R.)*, 10 Aug. 1774; *N.Y.R.G.*, 15 Apr. 1780; Inglis, *The True Interest*, 60–62; Seabury, *A View of the Controversy*, 19.

31. Calhoon, "William Smith's Alternative," 108–17; Calhoon, *The Loyalists in Revolutionary America*, 93–104; Sabine, *Historical Memoirs*, 246–47; William Sabine, "William Smith and His Imperial 'Compact,' " *Manuscripts*, VIII (1956), 315–18. Smith did not propose a specific number for the council, but suggested that "at least twenty-four" of the members be appointed by the crown.

32. [Jared Ingersoll], *Mr. Ingersoll's Letters Relating to the Stamp Act* (New Haven, 1766), 4; Lawrence Gipson, *Jared Ingersoll: A Study of American Loyalism* (New Haven, 1920), 127–64; Edmund S. Morgan and Helen M. Morgan, *The Stamp Act Crisis: Prologue to Revolution* (Chapel Hill, 1953), 220–37; New York Historical Society, *Collections*, "The Letters and Papers of Cadwallader Colden, 1711–1755" (68 vols., 1918–37), IX, 67; E.S. Morgan, ed., *Prologue to Revolution: Sources and Documents on the Stamp Act Crisis* (Chapel Hill, 1959), 55, 61; Sabine, *Historical Memoirs*, 29; Norton, *The British-Americans*, 3–7.

33. William Benton, *Whig Loyalism: An Aspect of Political Ideology in the American Revolutionary Era* (Cranbury, N.J., 1969), 94–95. The Loyalists were so divided that even Boucher, who is regarded by many as the arch-Tory, confessed on the eve of the revolution that "as things are now carried on it is not easy to say which side a real Friend to Liberty, Order and good Government would involve. For my Part I equally dread a Victory on either side." See "Letters of Boucher," 240.

34. Sewall, *A Cure for the Spleen*, 27–28.

Index